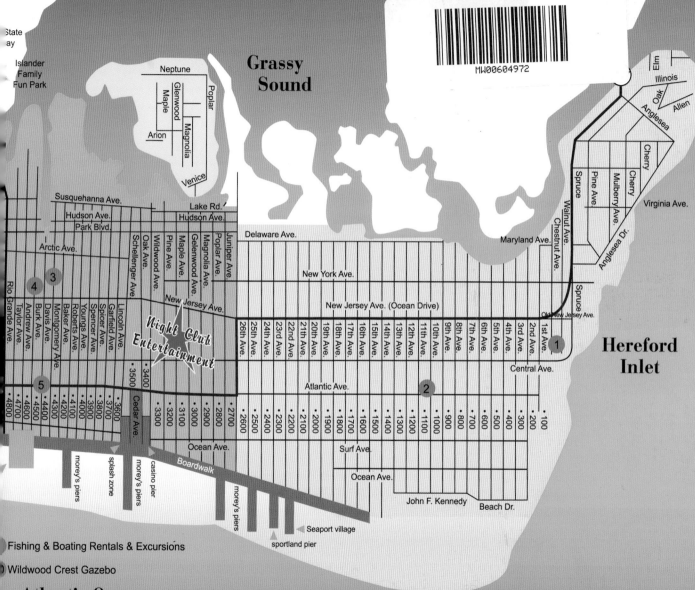

Grassy Sound

Neptune
Glenwood
Maple
Arion
Poplar
Magnolia
Venice

Islander Family Fun Park

State ay

Hereford Inlet

Elm
Illinois
Oak
Anglesea
Allen
Cherry
Cherry
Mulberry Ave.
Virginia Ave.
Anglesea Dr.
Spruce
Pine Ave.

Walnut Ave.
Chestnut Ave.
Maryland Ave.

Susquehanna Ave.
Hudson Ave.
Park Blvd.
Lake Rd.
Hudson Ave.

Arctic Ave.
Delaware Ave.

New York Ave.

New Jersey Ave. (Ocean Drive)

Old New Jersey Ave.
Spruce

Oak Ave.
Schellenger Ave.
Wildwood Ave.
Pine Ave.
Maple Ave.
Gelenwood Ave.
Magnolia Ave.
Poplar Ave.
Juniper Ave.

New Jersey Ave.

Rio Grande Ave.
Taylor Ave.
Andrew Ave.
Burk Ave.
Davis Ave.
Montgomery Ave.
Baker Ave.
Roberts Ave.
Youngs Ave.
Spicer Ave.
Spencer Ave.
Garfield Ave.
Lincoln Ave.

Night Club Entertainment

26th Ave.
25th Ave.
24th Ave.
23rd Ave.
22nd Ave.
21th Ave.
20th Ave.
19th Ave.
18th Ave.
17th Ave.
16th Ave.
15th Ave.
14th Ave.
13th Ave.
12th Ave.
11th Ave.
10th Ave.
9th Ave.
8th Ave.
7th Ave.
6th Ave.
5th Ave.
4th Ave.
3rd Ave.
2nd Ave.
1st Ave.

Central Ave.

Atlantic Ave.

•4800
•4700
•4600
•4500
•4400
•4300
•4100
•4000
•3900
•3800
•3700
•3600
•3500
•3400
Cedar Ave.
•3300
•3200
•3100
•3000
•2900
•2800
•2700
•2600
•2500
•2400
•2300
•2200
•2100
•2000
•1900
•1800
•1700
•1600
•1500
•1400
•1300
•1200
•1100
•1000
•900
•800
•700
•600
•500
•400
•300
•200
•100

1
2
3
4
5

Ocean Ave.
Surf Ave.
Ocean Ave.

John F. Kennedy
Beach Dr.

Boardwalk
morey's piers
splash zone
morey's piers
casino pier
morey's piers
Seaport village
sportland pier

Fishing & Boating Rentals & Excursions

Wildwood Crest Gazebo

Atlantic Ocean

WiLDWooD
By-the-Sea:
Nostalgia & Recipes

Anita S. Hirsch

"If the past feels good, why do they keep demolishing it?" – Michael Hirsch

WILDWOOD-BY-THE-SEA: NOSTALGIA AND RECIPES

©2009 by ANITA HIRSCH

Published by
Holly Beach Press
Wildwood, New Jersey

Library of Congress Control Number: 2009936453

Includes index

ISBN 978-1-61584-719-8

Book edited and designed by Jack Wright, Exit Zero Publishing (www.exitzero.us)
Cover Design by Dorothy Kulisek

Front cover photograph credits – clockwise, from top left: Rob Kulisek; Wildwood Historical Society; Wildwood Historical Society; Wildwood Historical Society; Anita Hirsch; Lake County, Illinois Museum (Curt Teich postcard archives); Wildwood Historical Society; Anita Hirsch; J.M. Currie of Vacation Time, Inc.

Back cover photograph credits – clockwise, from top left: Anita Hirsch; Wildwood Historical Society; Stanley Szczur; Wildwood Historical Society; Anita Hirsch; Wildwood Historical Society; Wildwood Historical Society; Anita Hirsch; Cape May County Department of Tourism

All photographs in the book courtesy of Anita Hirsch unless otherwise stated

Contents

MY FAMILY fell in love with Wildwood-by-the-Sea in the summer of 1965. We decided to drive south along the New Jersey coast from Atlantic Highlands to Cape May and we stopped at all the shore towns along the way to check them out. It was the Wildwoods that seemed to us the special place. Unique to Wildwood-by-the-Sea was the long boardwalk, more than two miles long, bordered on the land side by a variety of shops and on the beach side by amusement rides. We enjoyed walking on the immense, free beaches and on the soft, white sand. Ocean Avenue at night felt like Miami Beach with all the bright neon colors flashing at us from the large motels on both sides of the avenue. We hoped to return.

Several years later, we *did* return – with our young family – and stayed in Wildwood Crest at the Hawaii Kai. My brother and his family stayed across the street at the Saratoga Motel. They enjoyed it so much that they bought a small house in Wildwood Crest. After that, we visited them for a week or two every summer. In 1989 we decided to buy our own house

at the beach. We found one we liked in Wildwood – it was built in 1930, one of a group of bungalows with a porch in front and a garden in back. It reminded me of my grandmother's house with its footed bathtub, white porcelain pedestal sink in the bathroom, and white Magic Chef stove in one of the kitchens. Upstairs, off the living room, was a deck from which you could see the ocean and the boardwalk, only a block-and-a-half away. That was what sold us on the house.

It was an estate sale for the previous owners, Julia and Octavia D'Agostino. They had divided the house and added the second floor addition so that the single original home was now three apartments.

Their Italian heritage was everywhere. Inside the furnished house a 1950s Italian calendar hung abandoned inside a closet. There was a collection of saved string, buttons, and fabric for mending. An old metal hospital twin bed occupied one of the seven bedrooms. There were metal cabinets, not closets, in the bedrooms for hanging clothing. Overhead lights were in all the rooms, but outlets were scarce. There was a variety of vintage dressers and formica-topped kitchen tables with matching metal chairs.

Previous page: Sunset on Schooner Landing. This page, from top: the carousel ride at Morey's Piers; original Convention Hall front, showing Genova Pizza; goodbye to the old Magic Chef, which was one of many old appliances in the author's home. Opposite page: Anita's Place, the author's house in Wildwood; Kurtz Waterfront Restaurant (Wildwood Historical Society); the author's house as it looked in 1963 (Wildwood Historical Society); a view of the boardwalk at Magnolia Avenue.

Outside in the garden was a fig tree, chestnut trees, a grape arbor, and an old deep porcelain sink hooked up to the garden by a quirky connection of old water pipes so that it could be watered and the vegetables could be washed after being harvested. Old water pipes were still standing in the garden to be used to tie tomato and bean plants. There was an outside shower with a shelf made from the side extension of an old metal-topped kitchen table.

We purchased the house in 1989 and proceeded to make it ours. "We were guided by Julia's soul", says my son Michael.

I was hoping to keep it just like my grandmother's house: no phones and no TVs. But that didn't work. I had to call the plumber at the pay phone across the street. The answering machine commanded, "Leave your number and we will get back to you." Well, I didn't have a number so we had to go to the plumber's home to arrange for service. Eventually, we had to add phones and, soon after that, color TVs, microwaves, window air conditioners, a washer and dryer. We had to re-wire the house to provide outlets in each room. Now we don't even need a phone in the house since everyone has cell phones. And I don't know where the pay phones are located these days.

The Wildwood known by the tourists is a different one from the one known by the "Woodys" – those born on the island.

Simple Pleasures

THERE is Fascination to play, the Boardwalk Chapel to visit, bike-riding on the boardwalk, arcade games, the horse race at Nickel's, take-your-own-photo booths, and the rides on Morey's Piers: Giant Ferris Wheel, waterpark, roller coasters, children's rides, Merry-Go-Round, Tilt-a-Whirl, stuffed animals that are treasured and some so big you can hardly carry them or fit them in the car. And curly fries and tattoos and hair braids. Remember the waffles and ice cream, the square of three flavors of ice cream – chocolate, strawberry and vanilla. The sundae in a cone: the square ice cream fit into the special cone and then it was dipped in chocolate and a cherry placed on top. Two hot dogs could be purchased for twenty five cents with sauerkraut and mustard, too. And maybe if dad was in a good mood you could get more than three rides on the pier.

Woodys realize that the tourism business is what makes the town tick, gives them the money to make the town have what it does; but still, when the weather turns cooler and the town shuts down, the natives say, "We have our town back." They love the quiet. Driving down Atlantic Avenue without stopping for a red light and the blinking traffic lights on most streets are a sign that winter has come to the shore. In the summer, the traffic lights stop you at every corner. The Woodys enjoy the quiet while the tourists call the off-season bleak and depressing. The 250,000 summer population shrinks to 5,400 in the winter.

In the late Nineties, when the rebuilding boom began, people who had been in the motel business for years were happy to sell their properties and retire, so many of the motels were sold and torn down and condos were built on the sites.

On Bennett Avenue, where I live, the motel at the end of the street near Atlantic, the one that always took in the high school and college kids, that caused all the noise and the police to be called, was sold, torn down and a condo built in its place. The quiet owners and renters were welcome. The two-bedroom units were sold for $125,000 each and everyone thought, "Oh, they won't sell. The price is too high." But they all sold. Then the Candlelight Motel was demolished and the condos built there were priced at $299,000, and they all sold. Two more motels on the corners of Atlantic near Bennett were sold: the Blue Jay and the Talley-Ho.

Condos were built and were selling for $400,000 but by then the building boom was slowing and many of those condos are still vacant.

A boy and his father enjoy some quality time walking on the beach at Wildwood Crest

Many popular restaurants also decided to take advantage of the real estate boom and sold to condo developers. One summer we ate at the Captain's Table on the beach in Wildwood Crest and the next summer it was gone. We ate at Duffinetti's in Wildwood Crest that summer and the next summer it was gone. Another favorite was Kurtz Restaurant on the bay, with German-style food, wood paneling and a friendly family atmosphere – condos are now in its place.

Wildwood has changed and there are many people who like to talk about the "old days", when they were growing up in Wildwood. I enjoy hearing those memories of how it used to be. To many tourists, though, things remain the same. They still enjoy the beach, the restaurants, the sun, the salt air and the time to relax by the pool. Evenings are spent walking up and down the boardwalk, enjoying the shops, rides, food, ice cream, the tram car, buying a T-shirt and some fudge, saltwater taffy and a slice of pizza.

These days you can stop in to see the old Surfside restaurant that was moved from Wildwood Crest to Wildwood and is now the Doo Wop Experience, and ice cream shop. There is a new convention center that started a whole new building boom in Wildwood since the thought was

that it would bring in new and larger conventions, which would support new hotels and motels and attract new business.

The Fifties and Sixties music tribute weekends at the convention center are very popular, with thousands coming to hear the Drifters, Dion and the Belmonts, Fabian, and the sounds of the singers and bands from the past.

Visitors are always looking for souvenirs to take home to remember their time in Wildwood. And that is how this book started… a souvenir; something to remind us of the old days, of how it used to be.

Not that anything is wrong with today… it's just heart-warming to remember how it *was*.

THE Kechemeche Indians, a tribe which was part of the Lenni Lenape nation, were the first to enjoy Five Mile Beach. The land from North Wildwood to the end of Wildwood Crest is a barrier island within Cape May County with a beach along the ocean that is five miles long. An old Indian trail, the King Nummy Trail, led into the island from the north. The indians enjoyed the area in the summer: a place to "sun, fish, and hunt," according to historian George Boyer.

A body of water, Turtle Gut Inlet, separated the southern part of Wildwood Crest before it was filled in by the Army Corps of Engineers. When that operation was completed, it made the island seven miles long. The Two Mile Inn and Crab House was in that area, between what was Turtle Gut and the bridge to Cape May.

During the Revolutionary War the only naval battle that took place in Cape May County was fought at Turtle Gut Inlet between the brigantine *Nancy* and British warships on June 29, 1776.

In those days, farmers who lived offshore brought their cattle in flat boats or herded them to the island at low tide to graze through spring to the autumn. The first to live on the island were fishermen from Norway, Sweden and Denmark, who built shacks on the northern part of Five Mile Beach, known as Anglesea –

The famous W-shaped tree that even attracted the attention of President Benjamin Harrison, who asked to be photographed by it. Previous page: An old train station on the island. (Wildwood Historical Society)

these Scandinavian immigrants started the fishing industry. Hereford Lighthouse was built in 1874, after many sailors and fishermen were lost at sea.

The Five Mile Beach was often visited by those who were looking to discover a spot to rest, heal and relax by the ocean. Those who came were fascinated by the forest-covered area and wanted to develop the land, cut down all the trees and build a resort.

In 1882, Aaron Andrew, Joseph Taylor and John Burk looked over a section of Five Mile Beach and were impressed by the possibilities for development. They especially enjoyed the abundant holly trees. They duly formed the Holly Beach City Improvement Company, along with Nelson Roberts, John Davis, Thomas Montgomery, James Young, James McCandless and Harry Spencer. Their names were used in the early naming of

The Arcadia Hotel on Magnolia and Pacific. Right: The Hereford Lighthouse was built in 1874 after many fishermen and sailors were lost at sea (Wildwood Historical Society)

the streets, along with a few older Cape May County pioneers: Cresse, Hildreth, Bennett, Leaming and Hand.

The section denoted as Holly Beach reached from Cedar Avenue south to Cresse Avenue. The original Wildwood section of the city had streets named after trees, while the streets in the Wildwood Crest section were named after flowers.

The Baker brothers – Philip, Latimer and J. Thompson – founded the Wildwood Beach Improvement Company and developed the land that became the Borough of Wildwood (incorporated in 1896) and the Borough of Wildwood Crest, incorporated in 1910. Latimer Baker became the first mayor of Wildwood and his brother, Philip, was the first mayor of Wildwood Crest, from 1910 to 1920.

When the Baker brothers first visited,

the area north of Holly Beach was a forest of pine, maple, oak, poplar, magnolia, holly and cherry. One of the holly trees, in a park near where Wildwood and New Jersey Avenues are today, had a huge branch formed into a W-shape, which became famous. When President Benjamin Harrison visited Five Mile Beach in 1890 to cut the ribbon for the new Hotel Dayton, he wanted to be photographed by the tree. When the tree was taken down, the branch was saved and is now in the Wildwood Historical Society.

To get from the mainland to Five Mile Beach, a railroad line was built in 1884, connecting Cape May Court House to Anglesea. That train, known as the Mud Hen, had to travel across Grassy Sound and frequently got stuck in the mud at high tide. Then the passengers had to wait until low tide to get moving again. At that time the only other way to get into

"The Sea Toilers" in 1910; boardwalk in 1907; Wildwood Avenue summer cottage; entrance to Wildwood Crest (Wildwood Historical Society)

Wildwood was by an old wooden bridge from Rio Grande. By 1903, it was rebuilt and is now called the George Redding Bridge.

In 1906 the name Anglesea was changed to North Wildwood. Many at that time hoped to consolidate all the boroughs, especially Anglesea, Wildwood and Holly Beach City into a city to be called Wildwood-by-the-Sea, but a bill to that effect was defeated. The feeling at the time was that each borough should be allowed to grow larger before the consolidation. In 1912 Holly Beach consolidated with the Borough of Wildwood to form the City of Wildwood.

In 1870, Warren Hann, who was hired as the superintendent of the Wildwood and Delaware Bay Short Line Railroad, saw the possibilities of developing the marshland on Grassy Sound, west of the Five Mile Beach, and he founded West Wildwood. It is an island and has to be reached by crossing a bridge from Wildwood at Glenwood Avenue, which is the only entrance other than by boat. Before the bridge was built, ice was delivered by row boat. By 1915, cottages and bungalows were selling for $1000.

In 1889, the ocean came all the way up to where Atlantic Avenue is now, in Wildwood, and up to Surf Avenue in Wildwood Crest. Most of the homes were built close to the shore, from Beach Avenue to Pacific and from Burk to Rio Grande. A storm washed away most of those homes in September of 1889.

Homes not moved, destroyed by hurricane, flood, fire or demolition are few. Those still in existence include the Taylor House, which was moved to 126 E. Hildreth Avenue; the home of William Paul, called Holly Leaves, which is still located at 145 E. Rio Grande; and the oldest house in Wildwood, at 125 W. Pine, which has a large front porch and white-and-gold painted around the windows. Other old homes still in existence are 151 East Young, Bonelli's house on the corner of Pacific and Young, 223 W. Oak, and the fenced-in house on the corner of Rio Grande and Pacific. In Wildwood Crest along East Heather Road, you will find

The late, lamented Ebb Tide Motel in Wildwood Crest
Photograph by Michael Hirsch

some homes around 100 years old.

The first boardwalk was constructed in 1899, of boards that were laid even with the beach. Later it was moved and raised so that the water could flow underneath. Now the water keeps receding so the beach is very wide and the water barely reaches the piers.

Up to the 1940s and early '50s, tourists coming to Wildwood for the boardwalk, the beach and the ocean, stayed in rooming houses. They came by bus or train and they stayed for $25 a night in a

room with a bath. Or, for $15 a night you could stay in a room with a sink, with the bath down the hall.

When the automobile with the big tail fins was the mode of travel, Wildwood wanted to attract tourists who could come with their cars. The neon signs attracted those to stay. The first motel built in Wildwood Crest was the Ebb Tide and it advertised "air conditioning, a TV in every room, a sundeck and only a short walk to the beach." The Ebb Tide is no longer in existence but some of the signature motels still standing include the Singapore, the Caribbean, the Bel Air, and the Chateau Bleu.

Most of the motels were built between 1955 and 1965. By the 1980s, there were about 320 motels. which gave the Wildwoods a most significant collection of mid-twentieth century architecture in the US.

So come on "downashore" to Wildwood-by-the-Sea and make your own memories. Check out the living history in the Wildwoods, ride the Giant Ferris Wheel, the old wooden roller coaster on Morey's Piers, pedal a bike, see the Friday night fireworks, ride the tram car, stroll the boardwalk, buy some ice cream, fudge and taffy, see a movie on the beach, plant an umbrella, ride the waves and look for sea shells. And don't forget to visit the Wildwood Historical Society – they have an amazing collection of nostalgia.

Destination North Wildwood

By Dorothy Kulisek, Artist, Publisher and Editor of "Sun-by-the-Sea"

I T ISN'T the first day of summer in Philadelphia for the McMonagle family until the last day of school. When that last bell is heard, the world turns into one long, hot summer day. When I got home, my mother would hand out six brown paper shopping bags, one for me and one for each of the McMonagle brothers and sisters to pack whatever we wanted to bring to the shore for the summer. We all scurried as mom yelled, "We are leaving in five minutes!" She packed us all in the station wagon, along with the dog, while "See You in September" played on the radio. We waved bye to our friends, while we looked forward with unbearable anticipation to what lay ahead. Mom put on her driving sunglasses, hung her arm out the window and we were on our way to the Shore.

Once in the Garden State, mom pulled over at the first farmers' market to pick up some fresh produce. The girls are counting how many licks it takes to get to the Tootsie Roll in the lollipop; the boys are naming all the roadkill. We're getting closer when we start to smell the salt air and we spot our first seagull.

We see the big neon sign that reads "WILDWOOD" as we turn off at Exit 6 and join the long line of cars along Grassy Sound Boulevard heading over the rickety old bridge. One by one we pass the familiar sites: The Crab Shack, Dad's Place, Jim's Clam Bar, Ed Zaberers, The Shell Shop, the pink Lurae Motel and finally we pull up to our mint green summer house.

The pink-and-blue snowball bushes are blooming and the lawn needs mowing. We hurry to the backyard to find our rusty bicycles, fishing rods and crab traps where we left them last year on Labor Day. The sky is so blue and so clear at the shore and the ocean's roar is beckoning us to come near. We step up on to the clamshell-lined porch that doesn't have its yellow-and-white striped awning up yet and open the old jalousied glass door to breathe the wonderful, seashore scent of our beach home. We make our way past the mismatched furniture to the pencil lines on the wall and to see how much we grew from last year. We look in our dressers and pull out

The rickety bridge over Grassy Sound (Wildwood Historical Society)

Jim's Clam Bar was a favorite stop for the McMonagles (Wildwood Historical Society)

The McMonagle family's summer house Photograph by Dorothy Kulisek

Top: Central Avenue looking north (Wildwood Historical Society). Above: The pink Lurae Motel (Wildwood Historical Society). Right: Sharon McMonagle. Opposite page: Dorothy McMonagle Kulisek in Wildwood in 1968.

the musty smelling bathing suits from last summer and we unpack our brown paper "suitcases". The shades are rolled up and the windows are thrown open to let the summer back in.

My mom and dad purchased this summer house at 309 E. Seventh Street in 1967. They still own the house and are expanding

it and have retired to that memory-filled home. After I graduated from college in 1983, I spent the summer in Wildwood and I never left at the end of that summer!

It's these abundantly-cherished childhood memories of my Wildwood summers that make this island my forever happy place. Thank you, mom and dad.

Dorothy Kulisek's Chicken Soup

This soup is good anytime but best on a cold wintry day or when you have a cold.

1/4 cup olive oil
4 large carrots, peeled and sliced
1/2 stalk of celery, chopped
1 teaspoon black pepper
2 split chicken breasts
1 (48 oz) can chicken broth
1 (16 oz) package wide egg noodles, cooked

Add olive oil to a soup pot and heat. Add carrots and celery to oil. Sauté for about 10 minutes. Add black pepper and chicken breasts. Sauté for about 10 minutes on each side. Add chicken broth. Simmer, covered, on low heat for approximately 1 hour.

Remove chicken breasts and let cool slightly. Skin and cut chicken into bite-size chunks. Add chicken back into the soup with cooked noodles and continue to simmer for about 10 minutes until all is cooked through and hot.

Yields 10 servings

The Crest & Hawaii Kai
For the kids, it was the beginning of something very special

THE Jersey Shore, the beach and the waves beckoned our young family for our summer vacation in 1974. The kids were the right age to enjoy the beach: Michael was 10 years and Leanne was six years. We knew of the beautiful beach in Wildwood Crest and heard about the Hawaii Kai from cousins Herb and Stephanie Cohen, who knew Larry Hand, the owner of the

Hawaii Kai at that time. We were able to make a reservation and we packed up our Chevy station wagon and tossed the kids in the way back with the luggage – this was before seatbelts – and drove to the Shore.

We got off the Garden State Parkway on to Rio Grande. Just over the George Redding Bridge to the right was Urie's, a good seafood restaurant on the water.

Next, on the left, we noticed C.R. Fannies, a bar and strip club at the corner of Susquehanna and Rio Grande – what an introduction to the town! Before it was C.R. Fannies, it was a more respectable Wolf's Saloon, owned by May Wolf. It has since been demolished to make way for the second half of the Marina Bay condos or another project.

Continuing along Rio Grande we noticed the Tom Cat, a restaurant begun by Tommy Taylor which was originally a gas station. The Tom Cat opened about 11pm, stayed open all night and closed in the morning, around 7am. Growing up in

Left: Michael and Lean
Opposite page: A Hawaii
on the diving
Photographs

the Wildwoods, the place to go for a
after a movie or a dance was the Tom Ca
and an important part of the teen years.

Once we arrived at the Hawaii Kai, we
unpacked and walked to the beach. The
kids enjoyed jumping the waves, digging
large holes to bury each other in the sand,
looking for shells, digging for sand crabs
and making sand castles. We found time
to rent bikes near the boardwalk and had
a few early morning rides.

The motel had a small pool and
Michael dove into the water head first for
the first time while we were there. Leanne
took her chance on sliding down the huge
slide into the water. And she jumped into
the pool from the diving board.

One day Michael and Sy went deep-
sea fishing on the *Holiday* party boat.
They caught a few fish and cleaned them,
then cooked them in the motel room.
We had a kitchenette which we stocked
with juice, milk and dry cereal for quick
breakfasts. We did have breakfast at
Uncle Lou's once after renting bikes, a
serious and memorable breakfast spot.
Another morning breakfast was eaten at
the Saratoga Inn Coffee Shop across from
the Hawaii Kai.

Michael and Leanne checking on the sand crabs they found on Wildwood Crest beach.
Right: Anita Hirsch with Leanne and Michael in 1974. Photographs by Syman Hirsch

Urie's, a popular waterfront restaurant, as it looked in 1960 (Wildwood Historical Society)

We always ate dinner out. The Captain's Table was a great place to take kids for dinner with its views of the ocean and a magician who stopped by the tables with children to perform tricks or make balloon dogs. We also ate at the nearby Sand Castle and enjoyed a quick dinner at Mack's pizza on the boardwalk. One night we enjoyed the great food and antiques at Zaberer's in North Wildwood.

In the evening, after dinner, we went back to the boardwalk and walked, played arcade games, enjoyed the rides on the piers, eating an ice cream cone or some fudge or saltwater taffy. It was a fun and carefree time.

The Tom Cat today, still offering all-night eating for the Wildwoods' hungry visitors

Wolf's Café later became C. R. Fannies, a bar and strip club, which was demolished (Wildwood Historical Society)

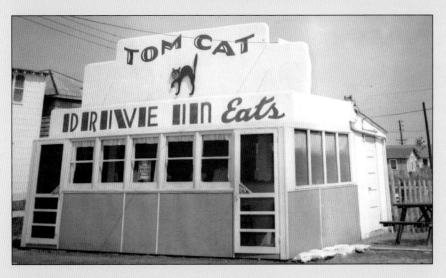

The Tom Cat back in the day, after it was converted from a gas station by Tommy Taylor (Wildwood Historical Society)

Easy Chicken Curry

Here is an easy kitchenette recipe that only needs a bag of salad to complete the meal. Quick or instant rice can be used instead of bulghur.

2 tablespoons olive oil
1 lb skinless, boneless chicken breasts
1 medium onion, chopped
1 tablespoon curry powder
1 Granny Smith apple, peeled
    and chopped
1/3 cup golden raisins
1 cup chicken broth
1 cup light bulghur
2 cups water
Chopped peanuts
Toasted coconut

Heat the olive oil in a skillet. Add the chicken and cook until golden brown on both sides, about 8-10 minutes. Remove the chicken to a plate.

Add the onions to the same pan and sauté until softened, about 5 minutes. Add the curry powder and heat for a minute. Add the chicken back into the pan with the apples, raisins and chicken broth. Bring to a boil, lower heat, cover and cook for 10-12 minutes.

Prepare bulghur by boiling water. Add bulghur, turn off heat, stir, cover.

To serve, add 2/3 cup bulghur on to a plate. Cover with a serving of chicken then some of the apple, raisin sauce. Top with peanuts and toasted coconut.

Yields four servings

Summers in the Seventies

Reminescences from Steve Lerario

WILDWOOD in the Seventies was South Philadelphia moved south for the summer. Kids from South Philly, who lived in the various sections of the city, seemed to get along in the summers in Wildwood. "Kids from 6th and Wharton, 28th and McKean, 9th and Reed, 19th and Rit-ner, 16th and Jackson: all these corners seemed to be in harmony in Wildwood," says Steve Lerario, who spent six weeks every summer with his grandparents, Rose and Tony Sckaruckarelli in their house in Wildwood on Bennett Avenue which was known as the R&T Apartments from 1956 to 1978.

In those days, the Sunshine Inn (now Dominic's Restaurant), a soda fountain and variety store on Pacific near the corner of Bennett, "was a place only the coolest of the cool hung out," according to Steve, who was about 10 years old then. Many were the older brothers of his friends, and Steve remembers admiring them.

Steve says that he and his friends "would stand across the street from the Sunshine Inn, at Putt Putt, the miniature golf course, now Duffers, and watch what went on. The crowds of kids, the music from the juke box…" It was a meeting place for the older teens before they were able to get into the clubs.

The older girls were like goddesses to Steve and his young friends and "the girls paid no attention to us," he says. "I did manage to get a hamburger in the daytime in there, but I would not even think of going in there in the evening."

During the day the "coolest guys and girls were all on the beach on Bennett Avenue, maybe 25 guys and girls, all hanging out close to the boardwalk, but on the beach." Steve and his young friends "were down at the water, body surfing, having mud ball fights, and eating fudgy wudgy ice cream pops with our moms! But we still

Steve Lerario's grandparents' house on Bennett Avenue in Wildwood. And, right, young Steve in the summer of 1961. (Lerario family photograph)

SFP 1961

had to walk by the cool guys."

Bubby, one of the "cool guys" around the Sunshine Inn, was from Nineteenth Street in Philadelphia. He had a big afro haircut, all the up-to-the-minute clothes, and all the "hottest chicks" followed him around. "He didn't look at me or my friends!" says Steve. It wasn't until twenty years later that Steve and Bubby became friends and Steve found out that Bubby was really Louis Marinara.

Steve and his sister, Susan, were able to go to Sportland Pool in North Wildwood for swimming lessons. Their mom decided to pay for lessons since she wanted to make sure that they could swim if they wanted to go to the beach alone.

Buddy Donohue, who lived across the street on Bennett Avenue in Wildwood, was one of Steve's good friends. Buddy was a mascot for the lifeguards: "he got to ride in their jeep." Being a mascot meant that the lifeguards let Buddy help set the lifeboats back on the trailers after they were used. He'd help get the boats out past the surf, and help move the lifeguard stand back from the incoming tide or up for the outgoing tide.

Steve wanted to be a mascot like Buddy and ride in the jeep, so he asked Buddy if he knew if any of the guards might need a mascot. Buddy suggested

Steve ask the lifeguard named Mike. Steve was finally was able to "get the guts to ask" and when Mike said okay, that was a proud day for Steve.

"Mostly, I ran errands for the lifeguards. I'd run up to the Rio Motel Coffee Shop for toasted cinnamon buns and tuna hoagies. They paid me two dollars a week and they paid me every two weeks. I thought it was worth it; I had a red shirt and a whistle. I bought the whistle at Scoops Sporting Goods (owned by Scoop Taylor). And I learned to braid kitchen twine so I could wear the whistle around my neck. I also put white tape around the part of the whistle you put in your mouth; I never did find out what the tape did, but it was part of the uniform."

Kona later took over Scoops before moving to their present site.

Steve wanted to wear a red shirt, like the lifeguards did. Rose Milani, a friend of Steve's grandmother, lived across the street and had a grown son who had been a lifeguard in Wildwood in his youth. Rose still had his red shirts that he wore when he was a lifeguard. Steve says, "Rose gave them to my gram, who made me go over and say thank you to Rose."

"The shirts had to be altered, so gram got right on it, but that posed no problem since she had worked in a tailor shop many years ago. In fact, on rainy days, she would show us how to sew buttons on scrap material to give us something to

Rosie's Ice Cream Shop later became the Sunshine Inn (Wildwood Historical Society)

Scoops Sporting Goods Shop was located at Rio Grande and Pacific (Wildwood Historical Society)

Steve Lerario in 1963 with sister Susan and parents Larry and Joanne (Lerario family photograph)

do. She taught us how to thread a needle, which now that I look back, was good to learn how to do. I think of gram when I thread a needle. Okay, so I don't thread many needles but the need does occur," says Steve.

"On one of our adventures up to the boardwalk, Buddy threw the one dime he had, on to a board game and it fell into the center of a Lucky Strike cigarette pack. He was the winner in that boardwalk game and he won the choice of the concession stand. It was a bear as big as us. We had to take turns carrying it home!

"That summer when I was a mascot for the lifeguards was a good summer. I remember a Canadian asking me if seaweed was some kind of plastic, as he held it by his thumb and forefinger and away from his body. I saw a man get caught in the undertow just in the gully right in front of the lifeguard stand. This area was called a gully snatcher. If someone was caught in the undertow, two guards were needed to save a person in trouble. One guard would throw the orange float and there was a line with a big loop that went around the guard's shoulder so he could swim the person in trouble back safely.

"Being on the beach every day, I saw how the guards helped the bathers. One day I saw a human chain of guards dragging the gully for a little girl that was supposed to be missing. The mother was frantic. It turned out the little girl was lost on the beach. Really young children would get lost on the beach a lot and the mother would run up to us in a panic. The guard would then call a Jeep and a beach cop. They would whistle the call from one stand to the next until they caught up with the jeep or the beach cop who could radio to each other.

"Those were memorable summers."

Pickled Beets

Steve's favorite cooked vegetable is beets. He usually goes up to a farm stand, buys them and cooks them. Once cooked, they can be cooled and eaten - Steve likes to add olive oil, sliced onion and garlic.

2 lb raw beets
2 tablespoons olive oil
2 garlic cloves, sliced
1 sweet onion, thinly sliced

Wash beets and place in a 6 to 8-quart pot with enough water to cover. Bring to a boil, lower heat to medium, cover, and cook for 30 minutes or until tender. Drain but save one cup of the beet liquid. Peel and slice beets uniformly thick - about an inch - or they can be cut into wedges. They can be cooled and eaten at this point, or add the remaining ingredients and chill overnight.

Place the reserved cup of beet liquid in a bowl and add the olive oil, garlic and onion.

Mix well and add the beets into the liquid. Cover and refrigerate until serving.

Yields six servings

The Sands Family

Making an art form out of packing for the beach!

AFTER spending a week in Wildwood in an apartment on Bennett Avenue in 1987, the Sands family loved it. They returned the following year and the following year and the following year. By 1993, they decided to rent an apartment for the entire summer: Mother's Day to Labor Day on Bennett Avenue, where they felt at home.

Friends and relatives rented nearby on Hildreth, Leaming and Hand Avenues and they would stop at the Sands' for a cup of coffee and to talk and laugh together. They often would meet on the beach and enjoy each other. They looked forward to Christmas in July on Hand Avenue.

By early May, Granddad Tom and Grandmom Mary Ann started to think about what to take for a summer in Wildwood. They packed up their car three times to make three trips from South Philly to set up their summer home in Wildwood. They took pots, pans, dishes, clothes, gas grill, TV and table, bath towels, beach towels, games, bicycles, boogie boards, beach chairs, coolers, umbrellas, and sand toys.

Tom and Mary Ann Sands stayed all summer but the children and grandchildren rotated on the weekends. Grandchildren Louis and Amanda stayed longer and longer; they didn't want to return to Philly with their parents. They couldn't wait for Mother's Day to arrive, not only because it was Amanda's birthday but because it was the beginning of a summer down the shore.

Mornings at the shore were for quiet time, sleeping in, reading and bike riding. Tom Sands was in the US Coast Guard and loves the ocean. He and his family all enjoy the camaraderie at the shore. When they went to the beach, they took a sturdy wagon that carried their food and drinks in a cooler, cell phones, iPods, suntan lotion, beach umbrellas, boom box, beach chairs, boogie boards: they knew how to enjoy the beach.

The only thing they needed was a restroom, which was right there at the Boardwalk and Bennett Avenue and later porta-potties were installed by the city, halfway down the beach.

They could spend the entire day on the beach and not spend money. The beaches are free... no tags needed. Set up the umbrella, chairs and blankets and hang out. The ocean, the sand, the seagulls and banner planes provided plenty of free entertainment. The Wildwood beaches

Mary Ann Sands' Peppers and Egg Sandwich

A Sands family picnic in the backyard at the beach (Sands family photo)

Mary Ann often got hungry for her peppers and egg sandwich, and was known to eat it for breakfast. The family also requested it for sandwiches to take to the beach. What tastes better than peppers and eggs in a hard roll or hoagie roll?

1 large red sweet pepper
2 eggs
1 tablespoon olive oil
1 hard roll

Cut the red sweet pepper into strips. Add the olive oil to a saute pan. Heat. Add the pepper and sauté until softened. Beat the eggs and add to the pan. Scramble the eggs with the peppers. When the eggs are done to your liking, cut the roll in half and add the peppers and eggs.

Yields one sandwich

are known not only for their size but also for their cleanliness and safety. The lifeguards are on duty until 5:30pm every day and you can set your clock by their schedule.

Grandmother Mary Ann enjoyed cooking for her family. She would plan menus and cook either in the cool of the morning or prepare something fast after coming home from the beach. On weekends, they would all eat together around one table: the family enjoyed eating her wonderful meals. She never felt that it was the summer and that she should relax – no, she was planning her next meal after the dishes were washed. Crabs and macaroni was made at least twice in the summer with her crab gravy. Pasta was prepared at least once a week. In the evenings the kids would walk on the boardwalk and the women would often play Fascination. After a walk on the boards, the family would congregate around the kitchen table or on the porch and play card games or Scrabble, Uno and Rummy Cube.

And too soon the summer was over and everything had to be packed for those three trips back to South Philly with all the equipment to store for the winter... looking forward to next summer.

Justin Sher and Michael Hirsch on the Crest beach in 1977

Down the Shore to the Crest

Making a barefoot dash for some special cheesesteaks

MICHAEL Hirsch and his family spent at least two weeks in the summer with his uncle and aunt at their home on Trenton Avenue in Wildwood Crest. The Sher family owned a three-bedroom house which was usually filled with their friends and family. Michael relates that the usual schedule was to get up in the morning, put on bathing suits, have breakfast and then pack all the beach gear in the car and drive the four blocks to the beach. Aunt Carole and Uncle Marty wanted to drive so they could park closer and not have to carry all the beach paraphernalia so far.

When lunchtime rolled around the kids would run quickly with bare feet on tiptoes over the hot sand from their position close to the ocean and make a dash up the long beach to the Reges Oceanfront Resort. There they served a lunch take-out on the beach side snack bar which served really good Philadelphia Cheesesteaks.

Everyone wanted a steak sandwich, especially Aunt Carole. She loved to eat those steaks on the beach and was awaiting the return of the kids with the food. French fries were always part of the order and they were smothered with ketchup – a Coke with lots of ice was part of the lunch routine. After giving the order to the attendant behind the screen, the kids would wait outside, trying to find a cool or shady spot while they waited. When the order was ready and their name was called, they would pay for the order, pour ketchup on the fries and run back to the beach to enjoy those cheesesteaks.

In the evenings, if they didn't cook a dinner, they would go out to Mariner's Landing, now the Bayview, or Monzo's (now Marie Nicole's) for Steamed Clams in White Sauce, or Mussels in Red Sauce over Linguini and Banana Cream Pie, or the Captain's Table or Kurtz, which was next to Jack Blake's Dock. (The latter two are no longer there, nor is the dock.)

Michael Hirsch visits Reges takeout in 2005

Philadelphia Cheesesteak

This is a recipe that comes close to what we bought at the Reges take-out. Make them yourself and enjoy them on the beach or anytime. The Philly Cheesesteak always is made with Cheese Whiz but outside of Philadelphia you can use your favorite sliced cheese.

2-3 tablespoons olive or canola oil
1 cup chopped onions
1 cup chopped green or red sweet peppers
12 oz thinly-sliced chip steak meat
10 slices white American cheese or 6 oz Cheese Whiz
2 10-inch Italian rolls
Tomato sauce or ketchup
Hot peppers or sweet pickle slices

Heat the oil in a large skillet. Add the onions and sweet peppers and sauté until softened, about 5 minutes. Remove from pan. Add the chip steak meat and fry until no longer red.

Place the onions and peppers on the rolls. Divided evenly. Then place the cheese on the rolls. Cover the cheese with the fried steak meat. Top with tomato sauce or ketchup if desired. Thin sliced pickles or sliced hot peppers can be placed on top.

Cut each roll in half, and serve.

Yields four servings

Sy and fish he caught on the "Holiday" boat at Blake's Dock; Marty, Justin and grandmom Mildred Sher in front of house

Summer Job Memories

All work, and... okay lots of play!

A SUMMER job at the shore... now that was a dream job. Not only could you make money, get a great tan, make new friends, enjoy a memorable summer, maybe even meet a life partner, but college students also earned money that could be used to pay for tuition, books and expenses. It wasn't easy to find a job because so many were looking. It was best to take a ride to the shore in the late winter to check around for both a job and a place to stay.

Deb Frymyer Croll remembers she decided to get a summer job in 1971 as a waitress in Wildwood. From her home in Ephrata, Pennsylvania she drove to Wildwood and stopped at the Wildwood Diner, which was open in the winter then. Deb walked in and was hired for the summer.

Making enough money for rent and living expenses as well as to help pay college expenses was foremost on her mind. She found a room to share rent with a friend but when she got there in the early spring she was the only student in the

Above: Waiting to have dinner at the Captain's Table Photograph by David Williams
Opposite page: Deb Croll as she looked in her orange polyester uniform in front of the Wildwood Diner.

Arky (Archangel) Guarino and Lori Forstburg, two Captain's Table hostesses in 1979. Arky worked at the restaurant after her two boys worked as waiters – when they stopped working, Arky took over as hostess.

rooming house and it scared her. As soon as her friend came down to work they looked for other accommodations. They found an apartment which they could share four ways. Only problem was, there were only two beds. They thought it would work because two of the girls worked the night shift, and Deb and her friend worked days. So when Deb came home from her seven-to-three shift, the night shift person was leaving and Deb could get into the bed. But she didn't really like sharing sheets so that housing arrangement didn't last long.

Deb "fell in love with working in a kitchen" as a result of that job at the Wildwood Diner. The diner was owned by a former mayor, Guy Musiani. His white-haired mother always sat at the cash register. Only she, and no one else, could touch the register.

Every morning when Deb came in to work she remembers the clean aroma of the grapefruit which the staff had cut in half and topped with a maraschino cherry and lined up on trays in the kitchen. The steak and eggs on the breakfast menu fascinated Deb: what a concept!

Locals came in for a doughnut and coffee every morning. Working the counter was tough for a short person like Deb. It was difficult to clean out the coffee urns, too. She had to have a stool to practically climb up into the urn. She remembers those glass cake stands with the glass dome along the counter. One time she was trying to serve a patron and move the hot coffee around the cake stand and reach over the counter and she spilled the coffee on the lap of the man and burned him… one of her more spectacular memories of breakfast at the Wildwood Diner.

Dottie, "a career waitress, ran the diner like an army sergeant", remembers Deb. "Dottie ruled!" The kitchen was kept spotless. Dottie ran circles around the rest of the wait staff and she was only about 4' 10". The popular song that summer was "Jeremiah Was a Bull Frog" and Dottie played it all the time on the jukebox. When Deb hears the song, she thinks of Dottie and the summer at the Wildwood Diner.

A job at the shore was also a dream

The Play Pen in Diamond Beach and, opposite page, the Red Garter... both were favorite watering holes for Lori, Kate and friends (Wildwood Historical Society)

for Lori Forstburg, who was a junior at Penn State University in 1979 when she headed for the Wildwoods. She and three of her Penn State friends – Kate Lada, Bill Doyle and Joel – drove in Bill's car. They found an apartment to rent in North Wildwood around 2nd and Central. A nurse and her daughter who lived downstairs owned the apartment. Upstairs was a two-bedroom apartment with a kitchen, bath, and living room – rent was $450 each for the season.

Bill got a job as a waiter at Zaberer's. Joel paid his quarter of the rent but they didn't see him after that. Kate and Lori got jobs at the Captain's Table Restaurant: Lori as a hostess and Kate a waitress. Kate made about $150 a night in tips and from that she paid the busboy 20%.

Lori learned all about the job of hostess from her mentor Arky Guarino.

According to Liz Skrabonja, another former Captain's Table employee, "Arky was the matriarch; the archangel, so we called her Arky."

Lori and Kate wanted to make more money for college tuition and expenses, so they both got second jobs: Lori worked in the morning as an activities counselor at the Crusader Motel on Cardinal Avenue, which was owned by cousins of the Captain's Table owners. Some of the other waiters and waitresses who wanted a second job, were hired as social directors and lifeguards at the Crusader.

Kate got her second job at Fast Buck Freddy's, a doughnut shop near their apartment. When the shop closed late in the morning, Kate brought leftover doughnuts for her roommates, along with some special doughnuts she made for them that were overfilled with jelly

and cream.

Lori and Kate didn't have time to enjoy the wide Wildwood beaches that summer. Lori worked in the mornings at the Crusader and then would go back to North Wildwood to change and rest for her evening job as hostess, which started around 4pm. The girls would either take a loop bus or ride their bikes to work from North Wildwood.

The breakfast buffet at the Captain's Table on Sunday was a popular meal for the vacationers. Lori remembers that the Catch of the Day was most popular in the evening. There was a broiled steak on the menu and when the waitress carried it through the kitchen door, someone threw an ice cube on the hot platter and it sizzled as it was brought to the awaiting diner.

On a busy night at the restaurant

there wasn't room for the long line of diners to wait inside, so the podium was placed outside and Lori took orders right there.

Sometimes the entertainers at the local night spots stopped in to the Captain's Table for dinner. Lori remembers the Platters came in one night. Another time the world's tallest man ordered scallops and iced tea.

After work, Lori and Kate went out on the town to various bars – in 1979, 18 was the legal drinking age. Lori remembers going to the Shamrock where they sold five beers for one dollar, and to the Red Garter. They never went to Moore's Inlet, which she remembered as being rowdy and wild. They went to the Play Pen at Diamond Beach and the Penalty Box.

She remembers enjoying ice cream at the Sea Shell Ice Cream on Rio Grande. One night they splurged and went to Urie's for dinner!

The Captain's Table sponsored a softball team for the employees, which was fun on days off. The restaurant owners, the DeFranscescos, also celebrated with their employees for Christmas in July.

Lori didn't need to wear a uniform as hostess but the waitresses and waiters and bus boys wore white shirts with the Captain's Table logo on them.

She remembers that when they had a day off, she and Kate usually slept, but one day they went to the waterpark to take some friends there who were visiting. What a memorable summer they had.

Cran-Lime Punch

These punch recipes come from Kathleen Frymyer, the mother of Deb Frymyer Croll, who worked as a waitress at the Wildwood Diner.

48 oz cranberry juice
32 oz apple juice
12 oz (or two 6 oz cans) frozen limeade
1/4 cup freshly-squeezed lime juice

Mix all together and pour over ice in glasses.

Yields 16 (6 oz) servings

New Year's Punch

1 quart sweet concord grape wine or strong tea
1 cup strained freshly-squeezed lemon juice (about 6 lemons)
1 1/2 cups freshly-squeezed orange juice
2 cups cranberry juice
2 cups canned pineapple juice
2 cups water
3/4 cup sugar
1 pint (16 oz) ginger ale
Orange and lemon slices

Mix ingredients together, except ginger ale. Pour punch over large piece of ice in punch bowl. Add ginger ale, and garnish with orange and lemon slices.

Yields 28 (1/2 cup) servings

The Jan-Dot Hotel

Meeting guests at the station, and trying to make beds like nanny did

THE Jan-Dot Hotel was one of a type of hotel that was popular in the Forties and Fifties. We would call it a rooming house. The Jan-Dot was on East Oak Avenue, right behind the present Bolero Motel and across the street from where the Red Oak Restaurant is today. Rooms were rented for a day, a weekend or a week. The second floor contained a long central hall, with rooms on either side with bathrooms at the end of the hall. On the third floor there were two large rooms with eight beds in each room. The third-floor guests had to go down to the second floor to use the bathrooms.

In 1948 Vincent and Olimpia Marsero decided to sell the grocery store they owned in Philadelphia to their son Frank and his wife, Dorothy, and venture forth to the Jersey Shore. The elder Marseros renamed their investment the JanDot Hotel after their two granddaughters. (There would be four more grandchildren after that!)

Janet Marsero Berman fondly remembers those summer days between 1955 and 1960, when her grandparents owned the hotel. Every summer, Janet and her sister Dottie would travel from Philadelphia to stay with nanny and pop. The sisters would also help their grandparents by assisting in cleaning chores, though they never could make a bed to meet nanny's high standards.

Janet especially enjoyed being told by her grandparents to greet guests at the bus or the train station, which were then located on Oak Avenue, and as promoted on the back of the JanDot Hotel postcard: "Only one block to the beach, bus and train stations." Janet and Dottie would meet the hotel guests and walk with them, carrying their luggage and packages to the JanDot. They might have to carry the bags up the steps to the second or third floors.

To thank Janet and Dottie for helping to carry their luggage from the bus or train stations, the guests tipped one dime, or sometimes even two dimes. The girls saved these dimes and spent them on the board-

Janet Marsero Berman and Gary Berman in front of the Jan-Dot Apartments on East Bennett Avenue. Janet wears an apron, just as Nanny Marsero did.

walk. Janet's favorite ride was the bumper cars, which was just up the ramp on to the boardwalk on Oak, and under the pavilion.

If the girls weren't on the bumper cars, they were watching the "pig" concession. A player threw a ball to hit a target and then one of a number of live baby pigs would emerge from a cage and go down a slide and hopefully enter the hole with the same name as the pig. Just watching to see if the pig went into the proper hole was an evening's free entertainment.

The girls' favorite foods to eat on the boardwalk were those that they could watch being prepared. One was the home-made potato chips – many minutes could be spent observing the potatoes being fried and then transferred to a warm oven. When you stepped up with your order and money, the hot chips were scooped into a brown paper bag. A huge salt shaker was on the counter to shake over your bag of hot and crispy potato chips.

Fresh donuts were made on Schellenger Avenue and the boardwalk, where there was a glass storefront. Everyone stopped to watch as the raw donuts were popped out on to a moving conveyor, fried and finally dusted with powdered sugar or dipped into melted chocolate.

Nanny would give Janet money to purchase six donuts to bring back to the hotel, but often Janet would eat all six donuts before she returned!

When nanny and pop sold the JanDot in 1960, they built a home on property they owned on East Hildreth Avenue. All the children, grandchildren and great grandchildren gathered there and still do, although pop and nanny are gone now.

Pop spent some time every day walking to the beach, riding his bike on the boardwalk, and taking care of the bocce court. In 1979, Mayor Victor Di Sylvester proclaimed the occasion of pop's 90th birthday as Vincent Marsero Day.

When Janet's husband Gary acquired a job transfer to Millville from Connecticut, they decided to move to Wildwood, where they had roots. They bought an apartment on East Bennett Avenue, just a block away from her grandparents' home, and named their house and its apartments The JanDot.

Summer Soup (Zuppa)

Once they moved into their home on East Hildreth, Nanny Marsero welcomed the family with a bowl of homemade soup, which was always simmering on the stove. "We always knew we were welcome or expected when we arrived in Wildwood and saw that pot of soup on the stove," says Janet Marsero Berman.

Nanny and Pop Marsero made the soup from whatever was on hand: could be vegetables from the garden, vegetables that were on sale in the market that week, leftover chicken, or clams that pop had gathered on the beach. The family legend goes that he used meat from the turtles that he found in the yard. The grandkids thought that the soup pot was the same large one pop used to soak his sore feet!

"Whatever was in that summer soup, it tasted a bit different every time but it was always delicious," says Janet. She always sat as close as she could to nanny while she was eating the soup, because then it tasted better.

Janet says "that on a summer night when the breeze is blowing north from Hildreth, I can smell that pot of soup."

8 oz sweet Italian sausage
2 tablespoons olive oil
1/2 cup chopped onions
1/2 cup chopped sweet green pepper
1/2 cup chopped celery
1/2 cup chopped carrots
2 cloves garlic, minced
4 cups chicken broth
1 bay leaf
2-3 large tomatoes or 6-8 Italian plum tomatoes, peeled, and chopped
4 cups assorted chopped summer vegetables (zucchini, turnip etc.)
2 teaspoons dry basil or 2 tablespoons fresh, chopped
2 tablespoons chopped Italian parsley
1/2 cup pastina, dry
2-3 handfuls spinach or escarole, washed and coarsely chopped
Salt and pepper to taste
Grated Pecorino Romano cheese

Remove the casing from the sausage and crumble into a cold soup pot. Heat the pot to medium, stir and allow the sausage to brown for about 5 minutes. Using a slotted spoon remove the sausage to a bowl. Pour out any accumulated fat.

Add the olive oil to the pot and heat. Add the onions, green pepper, celery, carrots and garlic to the pot and sauté until the onions are tender and golden.

Add the chicken broth, bay leaf and tomatoes and bring to a boil. Lower heat, cover and simmer for 15 minutes. Add the chopped vegetables, basil and parsley and continue to simmer another 15 minutes or until vegetables are tender. Add the cooked sausage and the pastina and continue cooking until the pasta is tender – about 5 minutes.

Finally, add the spinach or escarole and cook another 5 minutes. Salt and pepper to taste. Remove bay leaf. Serve. Pass the grated cheese.

Yields eight cups

The Candlelight, above, and, right, the Ocean Crest

The Candlelight, Ocean Crest and the Dutch Boy

Juggling with the demands of running a family motel

THE Candlelight Motel on Bennett Avenue in Wildwood was nestled in between the Windward on Ocean Avenue and the Eden Roc on the corner of Atlantic. Diane and Al Brannen bought the property in 1968 when only a single home was on it.

Diane's parents, Tom and Frances Panasci, owned motels in Wildwood so it was a business she knew well. Originally her family was from Buffalo, New York.

Her father, Tom, was a contractor and he built a motel on Columbine and Pacific in Wildwood Crest, which he called the Buffalo Hotel. He also built the Ocean Crest at Hildreth and Ocean, with 35 units and a pool. The Panasci family decided to sell one of their holdings and chose the Buffalo Hotel because it was farther from the ocean than the Ocean Crest.

Life was not easy living in their home in Buffalo in the winter and then, when Memorial Day came, mom Fran would go to Wildwood and run the Ocean Crest. Tom would stay in Buffalo and Fran's mother, Frances Singer, would move in to take care of the grandchildren until school was out. Then Tom took Grandmother Singer and the three girls, Candy, Fran, and Diane, to Wildwood to stay for the summer, before making the long trek north back to Buffalo. When September came and school began, Grandmother

hired a few sailors to paint the motel. That was how Diane Panasci met her future husband. One of the painters was Al Brannen from Philadelphia, who was in the United States Coast Guard, stationed at the Coast Guard Electronics Engineer Station in Wildwood Crest.

Once they were married, Al and Diane lived in one of the motel apartments on Hildreth. When their first son was born, and the house on Bennett Avenue near the beach was for sale, they bought it. With the nine units they added and Al's full-time job selling coffee to restaurants, hotels and motels, they were able to provide a good home for their two sons. Thomas and Andrew were able to go to school in Wildwood, play Little League ball in the summer, make many friends, keep their friends all year, and graduate from Wildwood Catholic, a path which Diane felt she had missed in her childhood.

Because of Diane's experience with the Ocean Crest she never involved Thomas and Andrew in the business because she didn't like that *her* mother involved her. She thought it was better that her children "pick a college and decide for themselves their career choice." Diane didn't think that having a motel was "a good way of life" to pass on to children.

Owning one motel is a lot of work, but later Al and Diane took over ownership of the Ocean Crest, and also purchased the house next door to the Ocean Crest

Singer and the girls went back to Buffalo. Diane felt her life was disconnected – she never felt a part of either town and she never liked that.

Diane remembers her grandmother, who emigrated from Hungary, doing all the laundry from the motel in the summers. "And in those days all the pillowcases were ironed!" said Diane. "Grandmother Frances ironed them by hand until she got a mangle to press them."

Whenever a grandchild was nearby, her grandmother would say, "Come help me fold the sheets."

The Ocean Crest office was downstairs in the back, and to the left was a room the family used as a bedroom. Often her mom would stop them on the way back from the beach and say, "Don't go in the bedroom, it is rented."

When Diane came to Wildwood the summer that she was 18, her mother had

Left: Al and Diane Brannen sitting on their front porch with their dog, Max.

Above: The original home on Bennett before any of the motels were built around it. (Miriam Clunn family photo)

Top left: The house as it was ready to move, in 2003, and as it is now.

Opposite page: Mother Frances Elizabeth Panasci and grandmother Frances Singer in front of Ocean Crest; and Tom, Frances and Diane Panasci in front of the Ocean Crest. (Brannen family photos)

and the Dutch Boy Motel adjacent to that. While Diane and Al owned and ran the two motels on Hildreth and the one on Bennett, you might have found Diane at home on Bennett or in the office on Hildreth. She would put a sign in the Bennett Avenue house that said: "I'm around the corner."

Once the boys were married, Al wanted to sell the motels, but Diane did not want to let go of the property that she worked so hard to keep. Their friends, Tom and Alba DiDonato, were contractors and they and Al convinced Diane to tear down the motels and build condos. It would be an attractive and useful way to restore the properties. But Diane still wanted to keep her home: "There were just too many memories to leave behind."

Since they owned a small house farther west on Bennett, they decided to demolish it and move their first home to that property. The move was expensive but it would have cost more to replace, especially such a well-built home as that one which was constructed in 1942.

Diane wanted the continuity. It seemed logical to stay on the same street. She didn't want to give up all things familiar. After the home was moved, it stood on the other side of the street, giving a different view from the porch. "It is astonishing," said Diane, "to look out the same kitchen window but see a different view."

Hungarian Goulash
with Chicken

This family recipe comes from Diane Brannen's mother, Frances Elizabeth Panasci. The chicken is prepared and cooked for two hours, potatoes are added and served over the dumplings.

2 tablespoons Crisco or oil
1 onion, chopped
1 chicken, cut into 7-8 pieces with bones
   and skin
Neck and gizzards (optional)
Water to cover, about 4 cups
Salt and pepper
2-3 tablespoons paprika
2-3 potatoes, quartered

Heat the Crisco or oil in a pot. Add the onion and soften and brown. Add the chicken and gizzards (if you like) and brown slowly. Then cover the chicken with water. Add salt and pepper to taste.

Liberally sprinkle with paprika. Bring to a boil, lower heat, cover and simmer for 2 hours, until the chicken is very tender. Add the quartered potatoes and cook another 30 minutes or until tender.

FOR DUMPLINGS
2 eggs
1/2 cup water
1 1/2 cups unbleached flour
1 teaspoon baking powder
1/2 teaspoon salt (optional)
1-2 tablespoons butter

Bring a large pot of salted water to a boil.

Whisk the eggs until frothy and add the 1/2 cup of water to the beaten eggs and beat another few seconds.

Combine flour, baking powder and salt (optional) and then add the egg mixture beating with a wood spoon. Mixture will be sticky.

Drop, 1 teaspoonful at a time, into the boiling water. Use 2 teaspoons and pick up a teaspoon of dough and then with the other teaspoon, push the dough into the water. Makes about 20 small dumplings.

Lower heat to a simmer and cover the pot. The drops will rise and expand. Simmer for 8 to 12 minutes. When dumplings are cooked, drain. Place in serving bowl and top with butter.

Serve goulash over dumplings.

Yields four hearty servings

Cookies Fun Shop on the boardwalk, and opposite, the Ship Ahoy at Ocean and Taylor (Wildwood Historical Society)

The Ship Ahoy Motel

Memories of magic tricks, and stealing on to shuffleboard courts

BRENDA Bortz remembers going down the Shore to Wildwood from Pennsylvania and staying at the Ship Ahoy Motel with her family. Often they would go with her friend Peggy Amidon and her family. And they all would always stay at the Ship Ahoy.

One of the first Wildwood motels, the Ship Ahoy was close to the ocean, at Ocean and Taylor, but the owner, Ben Schlenzig, was able to sell that ocean-front lot for a premium price, so he moved the motel back to where it stands now, near the Wildwood City Hall and next to the fire station near New Jersey Avenue. That section of the city was near the black neighborhoods of Wildwood, which was referred to as Brown Town in the Forties and Fifties.

The three girls – Brenda, her sister Nancy and friend Peggy – would walk to the boardwalk. Brenda remembers her "Wildwood passions: going to Cook-

ies Fun Shop on the boardwalk, where I bought magic tricks to try on my unsuspecting father; experiencing Entenmann's delicious baked goods for the first (but not the last) time. Oh, that French crumb cake: my favorite.

"I took my first steps on the Wildwood beach. At that time my parents stayed at a rooming house a few blocks from the beach in what was then the heart of Wildwood. When I was older – maybe nine or 10 – we started staying at the Ship Ahoy.

"My favorite Wildwood memory (along with occasionally finding dropped coins in the sand on the long path from beach to street) is of trying to sneak on

Coconut Cream Pie

Brenda's mom, Ann Bortz, never cooked or baked at the shore but when she was home in Allentown, she made a Coconut Cream Pie to die for. She also made an equally-irresistible Coconut Custard Pie. This recipe is a bit easier if the crust is purchased.

1 purchased pie crust
4 large egg yolks
2/3 cup sugar
1/4 cup cornstarch
1/2 teaspoon salt
3 cups milk
2 tablespoons butter
2 teaspoons vanilla
3/4 cup plus 3 tablespoons
     unsweetened coconut
1 cup heavy cream
2 tablespoons powdered sugar

Bake the pie crust according to package directions. (Generally they are to prick the crust and bake at 450 degrees for 8 to 10 minutes. Set aside to cool.)

Meanwhile, beat the egg yolks in a heavy pot with a wire whip. In a small bowl, combine the sugar, cornstarch and salt. Add to the pot with the egg yolks. Combine and stir with the wire whip and begin heating.

Gradually stir in the milk. Cook over medium heat, stirring constantly with the wire whip, until the mixture thickens and boils. Boil and stir for one minute.

Remove from heat. Stir in the butter, the vanilla and 3/4 cup of unsweetened coconut. Pour into pie crust.

Toast the 3 tablespoons of coconut by placing in a heavy skillet and heating just until the coconut is lightly golden. Remove from pan.

Beat the heavy cream with the powdered sugar. When stiffly beaten, cover the pie with the whipped cream. Then sprinkle the toasted coconut on top.

Refrigerate several hours before serving. Refrigerate any remaining pie.

Yields eight servings

to the shuffleboard courts directly across from the Ship Ahoy. Beautifully edged with flower beds at that time, the courts were free, but alas, off limits to those under 14. I got lucky often enough to keep trying and still remember the thrill of watching the red-and-black disks glide over the smooth surface, powered by long aluminum poles with rubber-tipped prongs at the end."

Time was spent lounging and sunning on the front deck of the motel as well as on the beach. Sisters Nancy and Brenda jumped the waves. Evenings were spent walking the boardwalk and playing Pokerino – and ice cream cones were a treat not to be missed.

Downashore

The Atlantic Diner

The names change at this corner... but the tasty coffee remains

ON THE corner of Atlantic and Burk, there has been a popular local eating spot for many years. What made it special was that it was open year-round for breakfast and lunch. It offered a good cup of coffee early in the morning, a comforting breakfast, a simple lunch, reasonable prices and friendly service.

In the Seventies, when my family first discovered the Atlantic Diner, it was owned by Barbara Waterman, who also owned the motel behind it. She always had a smile and a pleasant greeting, and enjoyed decorating the tables and the windows. For every season of the year –

Christmas, Mother's Day, Memorial Day, Valentine's Day – you name it, she had decorations stored away ready to display.

Barbara sold the property to the Days Inn around 2003 and Bill Mazari and Mario Montanero leased the restaurant. Before this venture, they leased the restaurant called Oceans in the Pan American Motel, and when they heard that the Atlantic Diner was available, they moved the Oceans Café there. You could see the old Atlantic Diner sign rusting on the roof next to the new Oceans Café sign.

Oceans Café French Toast

Bill Mazari, former owner of the Oceans Café, says everyone enjoyed his French Toast and he was generous enough to share his recipe. Bill used thick bread slices which he purchases in loaves called Texas Toast, and in the batter he adds vanilla, cinnamon and nutmeg, his unique ingredients. This recipe has been modified to serve six. As you can imagine, Bill prepared larger restaurant portions.

6 eggs
1 tablespoon vanilla
1 1/2 teaspoon cinnamon
3/4 teaspoon nutmeg
6 slices Texas Toast

Whip together the eggs, vanilla, cinnamon and nutmeg. Heat up the grill. Dip the slices of bread into the batter and place on the grill. Brown on one side until golden and then the other side. Cut each slice into triangles and serve each person 3 to 4 overlapping triangles.

Yields six servings

Opposite page: Bill Mazari, when he ran the Oceans Café, also pictured above. Below: Bob's Atlantic Café now occupies the corner of Burk and Atlantic. Previous page: Waitresses at the Hotel Adelphi–Witte from 1936: Betty Braidwood Taylor is on the far left and Evelyn Young is second from right. (Photo from Betty Braidwood Taylor)

Devoted employees and patrons from the old Oceans Café came to eat at this new establishment.

Bill and Mario leased the space for four years and then the lease was taken over by Bob Mulholland, formerly from the Aqua Beach Motel in Wildwood Crest. Now there is a new sign in the front: Bob's Atlantic Cafe. You can still get a good breakfast there with an endless cup of coffee, which is a comfort on a cloudy, windswept morning in the Wildwoods.

Britton's Gourmet Bakery

Continuing a legacy of freshly-made delights

I F IT is summer and you want something delicious to go with your coffee, you better get up and get in the line at Britton's Gourmet Bakery. The bakery opens at 7 am and most items are sold out by 11am. Everything they bake there is fabulous, especially the apple fritters. They are huge, and should be shared. Cut one in half or quarters before you get your fingers on it, or you will be tempted to eat the whole thing, or you WILL have eaten the whole thing before you know it.

While you wait, you can look over the two full cases of baked goods which includes all kinds of doughnuts, muffins, crumb cake, pies, sticky buns and Danish. Michael Britton comes out with full trays as fast as they are purchased.

Ray Britton Sr started a bakery in Stone Harbor in 1973, and opened one in Dias Creek and then one in Wildwood Crest. He learned the craft of baking by working at other bakeries and acquired some recipes from an old German bakery in Mt Ephraim, near Camden. Ray developed his own recipes, from scratch, buying only the best ingredients, and his bakery became very successful.

After he died, his wife Marie maintained ownership of the bakery and learned the craft. Now Marie works every day in the summers. In September she cuts back bakery hours to weekends only. However, pie orders are taken for the Thanksgiving and Christmas holidays. She often bakes up to 1000 pies for Thanksgiving.

Marie is able to do all this with her son, Michael Britton, and her friend Jack McDonnell. "The three of us bake, manage, and sell in the bakery." When summer comes, they hire students, in particular some eastern European girls who are working to attend college and they return for several years.

Marie also has a son, Ray, Jr, and a daughter, Marianne, a realtor, and five grandchildren, who can bake and have worked in the bakery. Three of the grand-

Marie Britton, Michael Britton and Jack McDonnell keep Britton's Bakery running... and irresistible

Walnut Bread

3 cups all-purpose flour
1 cup granulated sugar
4 teaspoons baking powder
1 teaspoon salt
1 teaspoon cinnamon
1 1/2 cups chopped walnuts, divided
3/4 cup butter or shortening,
    melted and cooled
1 egg
1 1/2 cups milk
1 teaspoon vanilla

Preheat oven to 350 degrees. Grease and flour two 4 x 8 loaf pans.

Sift flour with sugar, baking powder, salt and cinnamon. Stir in 1 1/4 cup of walnuts. Add butter or shortening. Beat egg in a bowl and add the milk, and vanilla and add to the flour mixture and combine until all is just moistened.

Pour into loaf pans and sprinkle rest of the chopped nuts on top. Bake for an hour. Cool and remove from pans.

Yields 2 (4 x 8-inch) loaves

children help out in the summers as does her daughter, Marianne.

Marie only uses the best ingredients to maintain the quality of the items she sells, which is especially difficult at a time when the cost of gasoline is raising the prices of many of the basics such as flour, sugar, butter, milk and the nuts she needs.

These days, most bakeries just buy frozen products and bake them, while Britton Gourmet Bakery makes EVERYthing from scratch. While you are waiting to buy your favorites, you will see dough being mixed and ingredients being measured and weighed. And you will be teased by the best bakery aromas!

On Fridays in the summer, Marie wraps a cookie and gives one to each child coming into the bakery to take to the beach – she calls this "Cookie Day For the Beach." The kids, in return, give her a drawing which she hangs in the windows.

At the end of the day, any leftovers are donated to the Eastern Shore Nursing Home or to the basketball team at the local day camp that Britton's Bakery supports.

Ocean View Grill at Ocean Towers

On the boardwalk, a genuine slice of Italian flavor, and hospitality

IN THE early morning, while walking or bike-riding on the boardwalk, stop at the south end, in the shops at Ocean Towers, for a great cup of coffee at Ocean View Grill. Sitting in the warm sun in front of this Italian bistro and enjoying the view of the beach and boardwalk is special. Panini sandwiches, Italian-brewed coffee, espresso, cappuccino, grilled ciabatta bread, egg and cheese on a croissant... can this be Italy?

Owners Celia and Ernie Caparelli met in North Wildwood just a few years ago. Ernie was born in Italy and came to New York when he was 11 years old. He married, moved to Savannah, GA with his bride and they raised a family there. In Savannah, he operated a breakfast and lunch restaurant called Ernie's. When his wife died, he came to North Wildwood to visit his father-in-law and took the family and the neighbors out for dinner. One of the neighbors was Celia's father, who she was visiting, and that is how they met – Celia had lost her spouse, too.

Ernie and Celia corresponded by email and married in October, 2004.

The Ocean View Grill on the boardwalk in Wildwood, in front of Ocean Towers.
Opposite page: Celia and Ernie Caparelli offer a warm welcome in the Ocean View Grill.

Penne Alla Caparelli

This recipe from Celia Caparelli appeared in the cookbook she helped publish for the Sons of Italy, Sylvester Grande Lodge #1838, called Tastes of Yesterday and Today.

4 quarts water
1 teaspoon salt
1 pound penne
4 tablespoons olive oil
2 cloves garlic, minced or chopped
2 zucchini
1 lb fresh plum tomatoes
1 tablespoon chopped fresh basil
6 tablespoons grated Parmesan
    cheese

In a large pot, bring the water and salt to a boil. Add pasta and cook to al dente firmness.

Slice zucchini lengthwise into thin slices then cut into julienne slices, about 2" to 3" long. Skin the tomatoes by putting them into hot water for 1 minute. Remove from water, cool under cold water for a couple seconds. Remove skin. Cut tomatoes in half, remove seeds.

In a skillet, heat oil and sauté garlic for 1 minute. Add zucchini and sauté for 2 minutes. Stir in the tomatoes and basil. Cook for 5 minutes. Drain the pasta. Add zucchini and tomatoes and Parmesan cheese and mix well.

Yields eight servings

Ernie sold his business and house and moved to North Wildwood. They decided a summer business would work for them: they could work hard all summer and then travel in winter and visit his sons in Savannah. Celia's children live in the Philadelphia area.

To get ready for the opening of their boardwalk business, they investigated various foods, coffees and coffee roasters. They selected an imported Italian coffee, and an Italian coffee maker. Celia, whose employment experience was in corporate public relations and marketing, decided that an Italian bistro concept would be the answer. The Ocean View Grill opened in April of 2005. It was a huge success: they were voted the "Best of Summer" for lunch in the Wildwoods.

The next summer brought some new items to the menu, including a crab chowder served in a sourdough bread bowl, more creative salads, a deluxe crab cake and customized coffee mugs.

They serve breakfast, lunch and dinner everyday and close at 9pm. When you pass, stop to read the handwritten menu board – you will want to try one of the freshly-made choices.

Celia and Ernie are never too busy to talk. After tasting the food, you will return again and again, not only to eat but to enjoy speaking with Celia and Ernie. They make you feel that you are friends.

Uncle Lou's Restaurant

The lines were long, but the food, and service, were worth the wait

A NECESSARY part of a vacation at the beach is eating breakfast out. Pancakes, French toast, eggs, bacon, sausage and a selection of toast and sweet pastries are part of the special breakfast.

There was one place that was popular in Wildwood in the Sixties and Seventies and that was Uncle Lou's at the corner of Atlantic and Pine. The lines were long but everyone waited patiently until they were called to sit. Nick Basos and his family were very efficient at handling the crowds that came for breakfast in the summers. They had their system of moving everyone through the restaurant. The person who greeted you would ask how many in your party and then signal to a person in the back who would see that a table was ready for you. Tables were quickly moved together to accommodate four or six or eight or 12.

It was a huge dining room, but

everything went like clockwork.

On each table was a metal holder that held six syrup containers that could be used on pancakes or French toast. You could have your choice of regular maple, blueberry, strawberry, raspberry or honey. What a treat to look forward to!

Before it was Uncle Lou's, the building was home to the Adelphi-Witte Hotel, which was bustling in the 1940s. In an article in the *Sun By-the-Sea*, Betty Braidwood Taylor remembers being a waitress at the Adelphi-Witte Hotel and Restaurant in 1934 with her friend Evelyn Young.

Breakfast was served from 7am until 10am, then lunch was from noon to 2pm and dinner from 5pm to 8pm every day.

In 1934, dinner cost 65 cents for a full flounder dinner; a steak dinner with a pound of steak was $1.25. And Evelyn remembers some patrons looking over the menu and then leaving because the prices were too high!

Some of the tasks that Evelyn remembers were part of her job were to fold napkins, polish silverware, fill salt shakers, sweep the dining room, keep the silver sugar bowls sparkling, and often cleaning the rest rooms.

The building has since been demolished to make way for condos.

Above: Anita and Syman Hirsch in Uncle Lou's
Below: Uncle Lou's was bustling in the Sixties
Opposite: Postcard of the Adelphi Hotel from the Ann Vinci collection (Wildwood Historical Society)

Easy Blueberry Pancake Syrup

Not only is this syrup really good on pancakes, it is also excellent on ice cream.

1 cup blueberries, fresh or frozen
1/4 cup maple syrup

Blend the blueberries in a blender until smooth. Add the maple syrup. Blend and serve. Note: if you want to save the syrup, it would be best to bring the blueberries to a boil after blending and then add the syrup. More can be prepared as needed.

Yields four servings

The Surfside

The rich family legacy behind a legendary landmark

I N WILDWOOD Crest, at the corner of Ocean and Lavender Avenues, was a unique building, round in shape, with an angular roofline and an aqua, orange-and-gold color scheme.

Opened on July 4, 1963, the Surfside was a monument to Doo Wop architecture. Tomi John had the idea to take on a group of silent partners to build the restaurant, which remained vital and bustling until 2002, when the motel behind the Surfside, the Waters Edge, wanted to add more rooms and needed to purchase the Surfside to expand their hotel.

The Surfside story really begins with the emigration of the John family from Macedonia, Greece in 1940. Dad Costa, mom Andigona, her son John Daskow, and their two boys, Peter John and Thomas Michael John, Sr (better known as Tomi John) arrived in New York City on July 4. They thought the fireworks in the harbor were celebrating their arrival.

After the brothers grew up, they discovered Wildwood and the restaurant business. In 1957, they leased Mullins Restaurant on Atlantic and Schellenger from the Hunt family. This restaurant, next to the Hunt's Shore Movie Theatre, became known as Tomi John's Restaurant. They leased several other restaurants in the intervening years, including the restaurant at the Thunderbird Motel at Surf and 23rd in North Wildwood, but always kept Tomi John's Restaurant. Open 24 hours, it was a popular place to start the day with Tomi and a cup of hot coffee.

Once the Surfside opened, the whole family helped run the restaurant. Besides Tomi, there was his wife Helen, their son Michael and Helen's children, Alex West and Bonnie Shaw, and Tomi's brother Peter. (Peter's son Philip owns the Sandcastle in Wildwood Crest, opened the Pacific Grill in Wildwood, now closed, and opened Jersey Girl.)

Washing dishes, selling papers out front, cleaning and waiting tables, and cooking at the grill – "You name it, I did it," says Michael. He met his future wife, Jeanne, at the Surfside when she worked as a waitress. From Chalfont, Pennsylvania, she came down to Wildwood to work during the summer of 1973. They were married two years later and raised their daughters, Krista and Lacey in the area.

True to the family tradition, Krista and Lacey also worked at the Surfside and helped to start the Beach Grill. They still come back to Wildwood to vacation every summer weekend with their families.

Top left: In the Surfside kitchen with Michael John, Ruth Godboldt, the cook for 40 years, and Tomi John. Top right: The inside of old Surfside, shot by David Williams on the final day. Above: The new Surfside West diner.

Macadamia French Toast

This recipe is not always on the menu at the Surfside West, but when it is, be sure to try it. Or now you can make it at home.

4 large eggs, lightly beaten
1/4 cup sugar
1/4 teaspoon ground nutmeg
2/3 cup orange juice
1/3 cup milk
1/2 teaspoon vanilla
1 (16 oz) loaf Italian bread, cut in 1-inch slices
2/3 cup melted butter
1/2 cup macadamia nuts, chopped and toasted
Powdered sugar

The night before, combine first 6 ingredients in bowl, stirring well. Fit bread slices in a single layer in a lightly greased 13 x 9 x 2 baking dish.

Pour the egg mixture over bread slices, cover and chill at least 8 hours, turning bread over once.

Preheat oven to 400 degrees. Pour butter in jelly roll pan, place bread slices over melted butter in a single layer. Bake for 10 minutes. Sprinkle nuts and powdered sugar evenly over bread and bake an additional 10 minutes.

Yields six servings

In 1994, Tomi decided to buy out his partners, but only three days after the deal was finalized, Tomi had a heart attack, and passed away on July 4. Michael became the owner and continued to operate the business with his wife Jeanne.

By 2002, the Surfside had 35 employees, many of them who worked for the John family since 1963. Ruth Godboldt cooked for Tomi John for 40 years. The Johns were ready to sell the business: they had been serving breakfast, lunch and dinner in the summers at the Surfside for 39 years, were tired of the long hours, and ready for a rest.

After the Surfside was sold, Michael and Jeanne John did retire but found that the restaurant business was in their blood. They purchased the Crestwood Diner, on New Jersey and Cresse Avenues in Wildwood Crest, which was built in 1963, the same year that the Surfside opened. The diner became the Surfside West: open for breakfast and lunch.

Eleven of the original Surfside employees signed on to work for the John family.

photo Rol

The Doo Wop Experience

How the community saved a Wildwood landmark

F YOU are looking for memorabilia to remind you of life in the Fifties and Sixties, walk on over to the Doo Wop Experience. Directly across Ocean Avenue from the Wildwood Convention Center is a quirky building containing displays of furniture, lamps, kitchens, Schwin bicycles, motel signs, rotary phones, and Zenith console TVs, collected by the Doo Wop Preservation League, particularly by board members Chuck Schumann and Paul Russo.

An interactive wall with a giant map of the Wildwoods, which contains a 42-inch plasma screen controlled by visitors and designed by Frank Nave, holds a constantly changing exhibit, inviting frequent visits. The map features Doo Wop music and motel information, and even allows visitors to design their own Doo Wop Motel.

A Fifties-themed café, the Doo Wop Malt Shop, sells homemade ice cream, sundaes, milk shakes, sandwiches and breakfast items. Outside there is a neon garden of old motel signs and a band shell behind the building is used for concerts.

The original steel structure was the architecturally-unique Surfside Restaurant, which stood at Lavender and Ocean

Above left: tour guide Mary Fox in her poodle skirt in front of the trolley before a Doo Wop Back to the Fifties Tour. Left: audience at summer Sunday night free concert Opposite: the Surfside resurrected as the Doo Wop Experience on Ocean Avenue at Fox Park (Photograph by Rob Kulisek)

Pigs In The Blanket

Joan Husband, a Doo Wop Preservation League board member, says, "In the Fifties, a popular appetizer was Pigs in the Blanket. If we couldn't get the little cocktail franks, we cut a regular hot dog into four pieces." Joan exclaims, "Don't forget the mustard!"

1 can Pillsbury crescent refrigerator rolls
16 cocktail frankfurters (or 4 regular hot dogs)
Mustard

Set oven for 425 degrees. Remove rolls from can. Cut each roll diagonally in half. Place cocktail frankfurters or cut hot dog pieces on top of each roll. Roll dough to enclose the frankfurter.

Place on ungreased cookie sheet. (If you use reduced fat refrigerator rolls, grease or spray the cookie sheet with cooking spray.)

Bake 8 to 10 minutes or until golden brown. Serve with mustard.

Yields 16 pigs in the blanket

Avenues in Wildwood Crest. When it was designated to be torn down in 2002, a call to "Save the Surfside" began.

"How can we let this building be destroyed? So much of the unique architecture of the Wildwoods is disappearing!" said Jack Morey, then president of the Doo Wop Preservation League. He found that it would cost $20,000 to carefully dismantle the building in order to assemble it again.

Morey made an appeal to the community to "Save the Surfside." The community responded with donations, and just before the final swing of the wrecking ball in October, 2002, enough money was collected.

The Byrne Foundation, located in Wildwood, believed that a museum was needed to define the Doo Wop period and they announced they would give a grant of $420,000 to restore the building. A grand opening was held in April 2007. Mayor Ernie Troiano thanked the Fox family, especially Betty Fox, daughter-in-law of the Fox Park namesake E.Z. Fox, for consenting to use part of the Fox Park for a Doo Wop museum.

Otto F. Stocker
Bernice (Morton) Sto

The Big Blue Sightseer
A crowd pleaser for 30 years

I N THE early Fifties, Otto and Bernice Stocker purchased a boat hull from which Otto constructed the *Big Blue Sightseer*, which they operated for about 30 years. It sailed daily during the summer from Ottens Harbor in Wildwood down to Cape May and back through the intracoastal waterway.

A chance meeting while ice skating on a pond turned into love for Otto F. Stocker and Bernice Morton. According to their daughter, Bubbles, "That pond is now called Pumping Station Pond, but was referred to as the Water Works in the past." Otto and Bernice were married in 1927 at the First Baptist Church in Wildwood.

Otto was the oldest of three children of Fred O. and Edith Stocker, who had moved from Philadelphia to Wildwood about 1917. Bernice was born in Rio Grande, New Jersey, the third child of Ella and John B. Morton. Ella was a descendent of John Howland, a Mayflower Pilgrim, and Aaron Leaming from the Revolutionary War era.

Between 1928 and 1946, Otto and Bernice had seven children and every one of them played some part in working with the *Sightseer*. Bernice "Bubbles" Stocker Lindberg, one of the daughters, remembers handing out flyers for the *Sightseer* and plac-

ing them on cars in parking lots.

Otto and Bernice moved several times in the Wildwood Crest area, and finally settled at 6000 Park Boulevard at the corner of Aster. The house had one bathroom and one bedroom. "Imagine one bathroom for nine people," says Bubbles.

"The attic was eventually converted into four rooms: one large room where the girls slept, two smaller rooms on each side of the stairs for the boys and a large room for storage. It had an old coal-burning stove in the basement. During the depression, Otto, as well as others from town, would go to the lower end of Wildwood Crest and

Otto and Bernice Stocker on their wedding day, left, and at their 50th wedding anniversary party in 1977, above. Opposite: the famous "Sightseer" takes to the water (Wildwood Historical Society)

collect coal that had fallen off the trains."

Bernice was an excellent cook and, during times when food was not plentiful, she would use her creativity to feed her family.

Pets were another important part of the family. There were cats, dogs, rabbits, ducks, squirrels and monkeys, many at the same time. The ducks would make their way across to the meadows to lay their eggs. Then, it was the job of the children to row across and collect the eggs, either for breakfast "or for mom to use in one of her recipes," remembers Bubbles.

When a local organization was having a bake sale, Bernice received advance orders for her sticky buns. Kathy Stocker Thompson remembers her grandmother putting her "hand in a tub of lard and throwing it on the kitchen counter with handfuls of flour and sugar," and from this came "the best cinnamon buns in the world." Besides her cooking ability, Bernice was well known for her knitting and crocheting. The children had homemade sweaters and socks and, when outgrown, they were passed down.

Otto spent some time with the Cape May County Party Boat Association, which was responsible for starting artificial fishing reefs off the Wildwoods to help the growth of sport and commercial fishing in the area. Otto spoke before the United States Senate to get this approved.

Bernice and Otto loved their garden. Everyone knew when spring had arrived and Bernice was working in the garden, as the smell of cow manure would fill the air. Bubbles remembers that "Otto would collect hair from his barber and place it around his plantings, believing the protein helped to grow his large tomatoes and potatoes."

The garden was centered around a fish pond that Otto had built. During flood tides and storms Bubbles remembers that "the fish and the water lilies were saved from the salt water by gathering them up and placing them in trashcans or the bathtub."

Bubbles is the family historian and fondly remembers their home and the family activity.

Bernice's Egg Nog

At Christmas, when family and friends would walk through the door, they were greeted with Bernice's signature Egg Nog. In the winter, the children would rush to the back door, where the milkman had left his daily delivery. They were eager to get the frozen cream from the top of the milk bottles. At times, this got them into trouble because the plan was to use it for egg nog.

2 quarts heavy cream
1 dozen eggs, separated*
1 quart and 1 pint half-and-half
1 cup powdered sugar (more or less)
2 cups Bacardi Rum
3 cups Southern Comfort
   or Canadian Club
Nutmeg

Beat heavy cream until thick, not stiff, then beat in yolks, add half-and-half and powdered sugar (to taste). Add alcohol and top with nutmeg. If you wish, beat the egg whites until fluffy and gently put on top for effect, then add nutmeg.

*NOTE: If you can't eat raw eggs because of the fear of salmonella, substitute pasteurized egg substitute. Otherwise, egg yolks must be beaten and combined with the sugar and half-and-half and cooked to 160 degrees to destroy any salmonella.

Yields 50 (1/2 cup) servings

The "Sightseer" pictured in the 1960s, and Ottens Harbor in an old postcard (Wildwood Historical Society)

The Sightseer, Part 2

Chuck Schumann's 50-year love affair with Ottens Harbor

WHEN Chuck Schumann was 13 years old, he began to work for Otto Stocker and the *Big Blue Sightseer*, docked at Ottens Harbor. Born in Wildwood – he was raised on Montgomery Avenue nearby Ottens Harbor – Chuck graduated from Wildwood High and went on to college where he majored in Oceanography. Chuck loves boats, fishing and anything connected to the ocean. His Uncle Bill Schumann and wife Mary owned Schumann's Restaurant and Chuck worked for them, as well as with Otto Stocker.

When Otto Stocker was ready to retire, Chuck purchased the *Sightseer*. Including the time that Chuck worked for

Otto Stocker, Chuck has been working on the boat for 50 years. Since Ottens Harbor was his home, he enjoys speaking about the history and story of the waterway.

Around 1900, H. H. Ottens owned the land around the harbor and his real estate business, the Wildwood Land Company, was located where Gus's Pizza Restaurant is now, on Park Boulevard. Ottens had the harbor dredged out with steam shovels to make it deeper and wider so there would be more harbor frontage to sell. He sold the 220 lots for $200 each for "wharves for use of yachtsmen."

Ottens built a home in Wildwood, which was later used as the Wildwood Yacht Club. Later it was bought by Lou Booth and became the Chateau Monterey.

Fishing was the important vocation and avocation in the Wildwoods. Swedes and Norwegians settled to fish and to sell their fish for bait and for food. Men came to enjoy the sport of fishing. They came from the Philadelphia area by a train, which came through Anglesea and stopped on Wildwood Avenue. There was a tiny hotel located at the train stop, only eight rooms, and men came there to stay overnight and to fish.

Among the original fisherman who came to fish to earn a livelihood was Ken Shivers, whom Chuck Schumann admired. "He was part of a resourceful group," says Chuck Schumann. "You have to admire them. They depended on them-

An old ice sign from old days when selling ice was important business on Ottens Harbor. Opposite page: Henry Ottens home, which later became the Wildwood Yacht Club and then Lou Booth's Chateau Monterey (Wildwood Historical Society)

selves... they needed to, because if they were in trouble out there on the water, and if they couldn't depend on themselves, they didn't come back."

Taking a walking tour around Ottens Harbor today, you can still see some of the old buildings that were an important part of the fishing industry surrounding the harbor. Across Park Avenue from the harbor was Russo's Restaurant that was family owned for 86 years, and recently sold, and rebuilt by new owner Chuck Burns, as the Ice House. Nearby, in the

Brass Rail, there was a still from which they sold bootleg liquor. During the years of prohibition, this harbor area saw business related to bringing in liquor.

The fish market is still there: it began as the Union Fish Market, then Carlson's and is now the Dock Street Fish Market.

Bars were abundant around the harbor, but most are no longer there. One had a floor beneath where liquor was stored during the Prohibition era. There was a Dew Drop Inn where the fishermen stopped for a room... an inn for travelers

Chuck Schumann was 13 years old when he began working for Otto Stocker on the "Big Blue Sightseer." Fifty years later, he's still at the wheel.

or for fishermen. And then there is the Ship and Shore Bar, where Loady Carlson, owner of Carlson's Fish Market, could be found enjoying a drink or a bowl of soup.

To purchase fishing supplies, there was a chandler shop along the harbor and nearby was a market for food supplies.

To send fresh fish to Philadelphia, railroad tracks ran from Anglesea along New Jersey Avenue to Rambler Road and then along Park Avenue to the Two Mile dock. A switchback engine brought the fish from Ottens Harbor to the main track.

There was an icehouse at the site of the old Anchor Inn at Andrews and New

The old house on New Jersey Avenue was the clearing house, where fish were checked before being loaded on the train. Right: at this house on Montgomery Avenue, boats and lines were repaired. It's now called Ottens Harbor Marine Service.

Riding the Sightseer on top, left to right: Jeff, Hannah, Robin and Lily Friedman and Michael Hirsch

Jersey Tomato Sandwich

Chuck Schumann's favorite sandwich is made with an heirloom tomato in season. This large flavorful, almost purple Brandywine tomato is cut thick, as thick as a slice of the bread. "And it should be eaten with a cob of freshly-cooked New Jersey sweet corn," says Chuck.

2 slices whole grain bread
Mayonnaise
1 thick slice of Jersey tomato
1 slice Cooper sharp cheese
Lettuce

Spread the bread with mayo and top with tomato, sharp cheese and lettuce. Top with the second piece of bread, slice and eat.

Yields one sandwich

Jersey Avenues that supplied all the ice to keep the fish cold.

On Andrews and New Jersey was a fish management office. In the little blue house nearby on New Jersey Avenue was a clearing house, where the fishermen came in to register a catch.

Mackerel were caught in spring. Scallop fishing does best in this area now since it is well managed. Because of the scarcity of fish, the fishermen catch fish that used to be thrown back. Now the fishermen go out to catch hagfish, which is slimy and long like a snake, skate and monk fish.

Mullet is still caught for bait, but by September 15 all the mullet have migrated south. Chuck Schumann used to go out at sunrise with his daughter to catch mullet, which they sold to Carlson's.

There were also boat builders surrounding the harbor. They built all types of vessels, including skiffs, which are small, light sailboats. One of the old boat builders shops is still found at the end of Montgomery Avenue – the little house with the cobblestone chimney was a boat builder's shop. "The owner had an old desk and in one drawer he had carved his immigration number," recalls Chuck Schumann.

Christmas in July
The East Hand Avenue Way

FOR more than 25 years, family, friends and residents of the 200 block of East Hand Avenue have celebrated Christmas in July. On the third Saturday in July, Hand Avenue between Atlantic and Pacific is closed to traffic for the festivities.

Houses are decorated, and tables covered with food line the sidewalks in front of porches. The odor of fabulous Italian heritage recipes fills the air: meatballs in gravy, sausage in sweet pepper sauces, hot and cold pasta dishes, scaloppine, subs, and pizza. Later in the evening, desserts appear – tiramisu, biscotti, cannoli – and everyone dances to tunes from DJ Jay Macrina.

Rocky Gianetti started the tradition after he bought a house on Hand in 1980 and walked to Bennett Avenue during a Christmas in July celebration – he decided to start one on Hand.

Santa always comes to Hand Avenue to celebrate with the children, but he never arrives via the traditional sleigh and reindeer. In 2005, the man in red arrived in Ed O'Rangers' green Chrysler convertible. For the 25th anniversary, Santa and Mayor Ernie Troiano turned up in a fire engine.

Santa is Richard Hassall, who sports his own long, white beard. According to Rocky, the children love the arrival of Santa. In their excitement, they run across the street, which prompted Rocky to file for a permit to have the street closed to traffic.

Since 1993, most of the planning has been done by Ed O'Rangers of 218 East Hand. Rocky helped Ed and between the two of them they make sure to buy and fill a pinata, apply for the permit, and put

The Serano family: Holly, Michael, Anthony, Anthony, Jr, Sofia, Amelia, Brandon, Danielle. Right: Tom Sands and his grandson Louis Frattari. Opposite page: Santa Richard Hassall and Hand Avenue resident Christopher Turco.

Christmas in July means that boats and homes along the bay are decorated for the parade that leaves from the intracoastal waterway towards Sunset Lake, past Schooner Island Marina, under the George Redding Bridge to Ottens Harbor, then into Post Creek Basin, back under the George Redding Bridge, and ending at the Lighthouse Point Restaurant.

together 135 little candy bags for Santa to give to the children. Red T-shirts with "I survived Christmas in July" are ordered and sold. The first year, the spelling of Christmas was an error but, says Rocky, "We decided to keep printing it wrong so that everyone will know it isn't the religious Christmas."

Ed died in 2007, but his children continue the festivities on their block of Hand Avenue. Friends, relatives and residents of the block all try to arrange to be in Wildwood for the Christmas in July celebration. It is a true block party and by the end of the evening, everyone is dancing in the street.

Amelia's Sausage Scaloppine

Normally Amelia prepares only half this amount, but for Christmas in July, Amelia doubles the recipe. "Some cooks slice the sausage with a scissors or a knife and some remove the sausage from the casing," says Amelia. Use it to top a crusty Italian roll or serve over wide noodles.

1/4 cup vegetable oil
3 red peppers, coarsely chopped
3 green peppers, coarsely chopped
5 lb sweet or Italian sausage
2 (6 oz) jars mushrooms
2 (6 oz) cans tomato paste
4 cans of water
3 to 4 sprigs fresh basil
2 teaspoons dried oregano
Salt to taste

Heat the oil in a large pot. Chop the peppers and sauté in the oil until softened. Cut the sausage into wheels or circles. Add to the pot and cook for a few minutes with the peppers. Stir occasionally until all the sausage has changed color.

Then add the mushrooms, tomato paste, water, basil, oregano, and salt and bring to a boil.

Lower the heat, cover and simmer for 30 minutes.

Yields 20 servings

Wildwood Historical Society
A must-stop for an irresistible slice of local nostalgia

I F YOU love history, you must make a visit to the Wildwood Historical Society on Pacific Avenue near Spencer. It was founded in 1962 and acquired its own building in 1990. They have outgrown the space and built an addition in 2009. There is no entry fee, but donations are always welcome. Inside you will find an amazing collection from the past.

Walk in and you might find President Anne Vinci, Vice-President Phyllis Bethel, Curator Bob Scully or Past President Al Brannen, any of whom will be happy to answer questions.

Historian and office manager, Bob Bright Jr, sees that all the information is well organized. He is a walking encyclopedia of anything Wildwood. With the help of vintage photos, artifacts and memorabilia, there is not a thing that he does not know or can find related to Wildwood and its history. He is the unofficial island historian.

Bob was born in 1936 and raised in Wildwood. He lived at 3906 Pacific Avenue with his parents, Millicent, who was from Cape May, and Robert Sr, who was born in Wildwood. Bob Sr owned Bright's Appliance and the family lived behind and above the store.

The building is still there, across the street from the Wildwood Historical Society. Later, Bright's Appliance was sold and became Sol's Dress Shop.

Bob Jr graduated from American University with a degree in Economics. He worked at Lippincott Publishing at 6th and Locust in Philadelphia for 11 years, where

John, William and Robert Bright in 1898 (Wildwood Historical Society). This page, right: the Wildwood Historical Society is a must-see for lovers of nostalgia. Opposite page: Bob Bright Jr, Buddy, and Bob Bright Sr, who passed away in 2006; the father and son appeared in a newspaper ad for Ottens Harbor Fuel Company.

Grandmom Rebecca's Sweet Coleslaw

Bob Bright says he doesn't have a favorite recipe. "I eat only what comes in a red box," he says, meaning his dinners are the individual frozen standards. But he does remember how he loved his grandmother Rebecca Henderson's coleslaw. Bob says, "It makes any sandwich special." This coleslaw recipe does taste a lot like hers.

5 cups thinly sliced cabbage
3/4 cup mayonnaise
2 tablespoons sugar
2 tablespoons water
2 tablespoons light sour cream
1 tablespoon apple cider vinegar
1/4 teaspoon salt
Dash black pepper

Add the cabbage to a large bowl. Combine the remaining ingredients and add to cabbage and combine well. Refrigerate, and serve.

Yields six servings

he was Eastern Regional Sales Manager. After working other sales jobs, Bob retired and returned to Wildwood. He volunteered to help at the Wildwood Historical Society for a few days a week – this was in 1982, and he's been there ever since!

The Bright family has a long history in the Wildwoods, in South Jersey and in Cape May County. Bob remembers so much of his childhood – name any family or street and he will have an interesting story to tell.

The Bright family were some of the original settlers in Holly Beach. Bob's great grandfather was Henry Bright, who had four sons.

On the Historical Society wall, there is a photo taken in 1898 of three of the sons: John, a lawyer; William H., who was in real estate, had been mayor of Wildwood, a sheriff and also a state senator; and Robert, a lawyer. The fourth son, not pictured, was Oliver, Bob Bright Jr's grandfather and a councilman for Holly Beach and a commissioner when Holly Beach and Wildwood consolidated.

Cool Scoops

Tasty snacks and treats in a '50s-style wonderland

I F YOU want to go back to a nostalgic time, stop in to Cool Scoops, a Fifties-style ice cream parlor in North Wildwood. Owners Paul and Lori Russo have an unbelievable collection of mid-century memorabilia. Paul takes the time to add to the collection and change the displays regularly. "He is always changing something," says his son Paul Jr. It is the kind of place you will enjoy and then return to with your friends and relatives to sit and enjoy ice cream while reminiscing.

Paul and Lori met in New York, where they were planners and interior designers. They moved to Wildwood in 2002 and purchased K's Motel on the corner of 12th and New Jersey Avenue in North Wildwood, which had been a beauty parlor on the first floor and a motel on the second floor. They transformed the space into Cool Scoops, which includes plenty of Fifties memorabilia, including an authentic soda fountain. Three of the booths were made from cars – a pink '59 Cadillac, a blue '57 Ford Fairlane and a red '57 Chevy Bel Air. Every corner is a feast for the nostalgic eyes, including the restrooms.

You can buy candy reminiscent of the past, including root beer barrels, Baby Ruth, Necco Wafers, candy buttons, Black Crows, Good & Plenty, Goldenberg's Peanut Chews, and wax bottles. Enjoy an ice cream sundae or ice cream soda or a cone, sit in a vintage car, or walk around and enjoy the remarkable collection.

Lori and Paul ventured down to Wild-

Pink Cadillac and Ford Fairlane booths inside Cool Scoops; the original K's Motel. Opposite page: Lori and Paul with Elvis.

wood from New York because her parents, George and Carol Capua, owned the Florentine Motel at 19th and Surf since 1993. Before that, they had been living on Long Island, where they raised their children.

Lori's grandma, Marguerite Capua, came to North Wildwood in the early Seventies and bought the Cape Isle Court Apartments at 9th Street in North Wildwood. Of her four daughters and four sons, all except two of her children are in North Wildwood. Son Billy and his

wife Karen still own the Cape Isle Court Apartments. Son Bobby owns Jurassic Adventure Golf. Daughter Patti owns Patti's Party World on Route 9, daughter Joan owns Aloha Motel at 3rd and Kennedy, and daughter Marguerite owns Alante Motel.

The Russos have two children. Their son, Paul, graduated from Wildwood Catholic and attends Rowan University, and their daughter Ashley attends Wildwood Catholic. You will find them at Cool Scoops in the summer.

Paulie's Cheesecake

Paul says it was this cheesecake that he made for Lori in a heart shape that convinced her to marry him.

CRUST
1 cup graham cracker crumbs
1 cup sugar
4-5 tablespoons margarine or butter

CHEESECAKE
3 (8 oz) packages cream cheese
1 cup sugar
4 medium eggs
1 pint sour cream
2 tablespoons flour
2 teaspoons vanilla extract
1 teaspoon lemon juice
1 cup heavy cream

Preheat oven to 325 degrees. Grease or spray a 10-inch pan. Melt butter on low. Add cracker crumbs, sugar and combine. Press mixture into bottom of pan and put in freezer until cheesecake ingredients are mixed.

In a large bowl combine cheesecake ingredients in order listed. Leave the cream cheese out of the refrigerator until soft: it mixes easier.

Pour cheesecake mixture into crust in the pan. Bake for 20 minutes lower heat to 300F and bake for 40 minutes. Turn oven off and leave cake in for an hour. Take cake out and let cool for an hour. Refrigerate.

Yields 12-16 servings

Before it was Duffer's, this corner was at one time occupied by the Sea Spray restaurant, which was owned by Mario Bove (Wildwood Historical Society)

Duffer's

Trains, teddy bears, mini golf... all this and some good food, too!

DUFFER'S is a wonderful neighborhood family destination at the shore: there is breakfast, lunch and dinner served in a dining room, with an electric train running around the ceiling perimeter and a toy bear balancing on a wire that goes back and forth through one of the dining spaces. To keep you busy while waiting for a table, there is a gift shop, and an arcade. There is a miniature golf course, which was voted Best Miniature Golf by *South Jersey* magazine in 2006. The ice cream to eat in or take out is homemade and if the flavor is cheesecake or cookie dough, then the cookie dough and the cheesecake are made on the premises also.

The brownies and the pound cake served in the dining room are also made from scratch. Anything they can make, they do. "Even the rum raisins," says Don Long Sr, are mixed by the staff. "Only the best ingredients are used. The vanilla is the best quality, the pecans are from Georgia, and the pistachios are from California."

In 1972, Don, a Wildwood native, bought a custard business on Pacific between Hildreth and Bennett Avenues. He leased it out for two years and then opened it himself in 1974. Besides the custard sales from an outside window, there was a miniature golf course on the site, which he renamed Duffer's Challenge. Inside there were 15 golf game machines. The custard stand had tables in front but it was open to the weather so he decided to put an awning over the tables – eventually the restaurant was enlarged and enclosed. The patrons who were waiting for ice cream or tables were

Ollie Snelling, Selena Kwan, Anita, Sy and Michael Hirsch enjoying sundaes at Duffer's; Rachel Costin and Lily Friedman at the arcade; the famous pelicans overlook the miniature golf

then able to stand under that awning for cover.

Later, the arcade was enlarged. When the bigger, more space-hungry games became a thing of the past and video games began, Don brought in Pong and then Pac Man. These machines were a hit with the kids who love getting winning tickets and picking out prizes.

The business is now a family affair. Don's wife, Dorothy, runs the gift shop. They have formed a partnership with their two sons, Don Jr and Douglas, and his wife Regina.

Regina is the manager and does all

Grandpa Feldt's Swedish Pancakes (Crepes)

Grandpa Feldt came to Wildwood from Sweden. His daughter Dorothy Feldt married Don Long, who went into the clam business with his father-in-law. After they sold that business, Don bought Duffer's. Grandpa Feldt used this recipe when he made pancakes. Regina Long still has his pan, which divides into 8 triangles and each triangle is turned individually. You can use an 8-inch non-stick pan.

5 eggs
1/2 cup milk
1/2 cup water
1/2 teaspoon salt
2 1/2 tablespoons sugar
1 1/4 cups flour
2 1/2 tablespoons melted butter
Lingonberries or sliced strawberries
Confectioner's sugar

Combine eggs, milk, water. Add salt, sugar. Slowly add flour and melted butter. Heat a non-stick 8-inch pan or crepe pan. Coat with butter and cover the bottom with a thin coat of batter. When edges become golden brown, turn and brown the other side.

Per serving: 4 crepes which are rolled and served with a dollop of butter, lingonberries or sliced strawberries and confectioner's sugar.

Yields 16-20 crepes

Duffer's cook Danny Pagan whips up some Swedish Crepes, pictured left in all their glory Photos by Aleksey Moryakov

the hiring and firing, scheduling, and game room ticket redemption plan. She also goes to pick out the prizes that are dispersed in the game room. One or several members of the family are always on the premises. Regina and Doug's children also work in the summers at Duffer's and are envisioning a business that they can go into together.

Outside, on the roof, next to the miniature golf course are three pelicans that sing a song. The neighbors don't enjoy hearing the song over and over through the summer so the volume has been turned down, but here is what they sing:

We're the pelicans
We're the pelicans
We have golf balls in our beaks
Cause our beaks hold more than pelicans
We're the pelicans.
Just ask us and we drop golf balls
Thank Heavens you don't need a cannonball
It is nice to be a pelican cause our beaks hold more than a pelican
We're the pelicans
We're the pelicans

Brothers Ben and Vic (Bubbie) at the back of their house, at Hand and Arctic, in 1947

On the boardwalk in 1945: Dad, Vic Sr, in rear and in front Bubbie, Ben and Lu

Sea Shell Ice Cream

100 years of the DiSilvestro/Di Sylvester family

A HISTORY of the Sea Shell Ice Cream Shop at the corner of Atlantic and Rio Grande in Wildwood has to start with the DiSilvestro family, who have been a part of Wildwood for five generations or almost 100 years. Letitia and Raphael DiSilvestro married in Italy – in Larado, in the Abbruzzi area near the Adriatic Sea. They decided to emigrate to Philadelphia in 1906 where they had cousins who sponsored them. Raphael worked as a masonry contractor. One of his jobs brought him to Holly Beach and when Raphael saw the ocean he went back to his wife in Philadelphia and said he found the perfect place by the sea for them to live.

So Letitia and Raphael came to Wildwood in 1909, where Raphael built a duplex at Hand and Arctic Avenues and rented out one half. This house was in the Italian section of Wildwood whose boundaries were from Taylor to Hildreth and Park to New Jersey Avenues. It was a safe neighborhood where no one locked their doors, and kitchens were always open to guests.

Life in the DiSilvestro household was full of fun and family. Raphael worked for the Wilson Dairy, which was taken over in 1945 by Abbotts Dairy. Letitia and Raphael's seven children were born in Wildwood: Mamie, Molly, Ralph, Victor, Lena, Mary and Harry. Harry D., a son of Harry Sr, recalls that to make money in

Vic Jr (Bubbie) Di Sylvester in 1957 on the Wildwood boardwalk between Cedar and Schellenger

Catherine Versaggi Di Sylvester at the Arctic and Hand "homestead" in May of 1944

Vic Di Sylvester as Mayor of Wildwood – he was sworn in in 1984 and served on other local and county boards

the summer the kids were told to pack up their clothing and sleep in the attic, which was divided into two large rooms. Their bedrooms were then rented for $5 a week to women students from Penn State who worked in Wildwood in the summer.

Their son Victor married Catherine Versaggi from North Wildwood. Victor and Catherine moved to the Arctic and Hand "homestead" and shared the duplex with Vic's brother Harry and his family. Catherine Versaggi also came from a family of seven children. The Versaggi Construction Company and Bennie's Café at 17th Street in North Wildwood (now

Owen's Pub) were the family businesses. Everyone in both families worked at Bennie's Cafe at one time or another. Vic Jr remembers his dad worked there, during the taproom era of the Forties when "a plate of spaghetti was $1."

One day, the story goes, Victor Sr got annoyed with the mail deliveries. Letters and bills always got intermingled, and mail had to be sorted between the houses,

so Vic Sr said, "I am changing my name to Di Sylvester," which is how two brothers have a different last name.

However... there is another theory. Vic Jr says that when his father attended St Ann's School, the nuns called him Di Sylvester instead of DiSilvestro. The name stuck and Lucille, Victor Jr and Sebastian Bennie "Ben" became Di Sylvesters.

Victor Di Sylvester Sr, or "Tootie" as he was called, was a shoemaker and he presented shoeshine kits with bootblacks to his sons and nephews. In the summer, the boys would scatter on the streets of Wildwood to shine shoes for 25c a shine.

Any money they earned had to be brought home and put into the jar to use for school clothes. When September arrived, they would all go to South Philly to the Italian section to buy new clothes. One day when Harry D. was out shining shoes, a shoe was put on his bootblack to shine. And when Harry D. looked up, the shoe belonged to Johnny Mathis, who at that time was 19 years old. "He gave me a $5 tip", remembers Harry D.

Vic Jr, known to the family as Bubbie, says that dinner at home meant pasta every Tuesday, Thursday and Sunday nights: "That was a dinner that would stick to your ribs." Tuesday and Thursday were spaghetti nights, and Sunday was macaroni night. Vic says he could "pick out mom's gravy" at any family buffet. "There was always a pot of gravy and a pot of meatballs on the stove" when he came home from school. He'd dip into both pots with a wooden spoon and place some of each on to a slice of bread. "What a great after-school snack: our comfort food."

Vic's early career was marketing and traveling for Dunn and Bradstreet and later promoting and developing manuscript ideas for college textbooks around the USA. After eight years, he got tired of traveling and bought the Sea Shell Motel

The corner of Rio Grande and Atlantic Avenue – the house on the right, built in 1900, is still standing
(Photographs from the Di Sylvester family and Sea Shell Ice Cream)

Blaine's Flounder

Marcia Di Sylvester is an excellent cook and collector of recipes and recipe books. Here is one recipe that she got from Coleen DiSilvestro which is a family favorite. Tilapia or any other favorite white fish, can also be used.

1 lb flounder filets
3 tablespoons mayonnaise
3 tablespoons grated Parmesan
   cheese
3 tablespoons fresh or dried
   chopped chives
1 tablespoon white wine
   Worcestershire marinade

Wash and place the flounder in a baking dish. Combine the next 4 ingredients and spoon over the fish.

Bake at 400 degrees for 20 minutes.

Yields four servings

in Wildwood in 1975 with a partner, Sam Rosso. They built more units across the street and then in 1976 opened Sea Shell Ice Cream. They used Sam Rosso's house, which he had built in 1950 at the corner of Atlantic and Rio Grande as their ice cream parlor. It was the first all-ice cream business in the area. Sam Rosso continued to sell ice cream on the beach from 1954 to 1979.

In 1980, Vic was elected as Chairman of the Wildwood Charter Commission and led the campaign to change the form of government of Wildwood to a mayor/council type. In 1983, Vic ran for council, won and became President of Council. In 1984, he was sworn in as the Mayor of Wildwood. In 1988, he was appointed Director of Tourism, Economic Development and Airport Operations for Cape May County, a position he held until 1995.

The Sea Shell businesses was sold in 1997. Vic and his wife Marcia live in Florida in the winter, but still come up to Wildwood in the summers to visit his many family and friends.

Wildwood Civic Club

Originally home to the first-ever mayor of Wildwood

N A previous life the Wildwood Civic Club was the home of Jacob Thompson Baker, the first mayor of Wildwood. In 1996, the house at Maple and Atlantic was placed on the NJ State Register of Historic Houses and also on the National Register of Historic Houses.

When the house was built in 1904 the ocean came up farther and there were no buildings to get in the way of the view from the porch. The original owners were able to sit on the side porch and could have an unobstructed view of the ocean.

The home has 12 rooms in it, and out-side an unusual columned portico with curved steps leading to the large porch and front door. Next door to it had been the Thomas Martindale house, built by a friend of the Bakers. That home is no longer there.

J. Thompson Baker came to Wildwood in the 1800s with his two brothers, Phillip and Latimer. The Baker brothers saw the wide beaches, felt the ocean breezes and could visualize the possibilities of the land. First they cleared all the trees, especially the Holly trees that were abundant, and

The J. Thompson Baker house, on Maple and Atlantic, is now home to Wildwood Civic Club. Right, J. Thompson Baker, whose house is pictured opposite page. (Wildwood Historical Society)

then they planned the town. They formed the Holly Beach Improvement Company in 1885 and, later, Wildwood Beach Improvement Company. There were still trees on the lots farther north so they named those streets after trees: Oak, Maple, Cedar and Poplar. They filled in lakes and named the two areas Holly Beach and Wildwood.

In 1912, Holly Beach and the Borough of Wildwood were combined and formally established as the city of Wildwood. J. Thompson Baker was the first mayor of Wildwood.

In 1913, J. Thompson was elected to Congress and traveled to Washington. He made friends with President Woodrow Wilson, who visited J. Thompson in his beautiful seaside home. Other guests at the Baker home were Champ Clark, then speaker of the House of Representatives, Anna Howard Shaw, the first President of the National Women's Suffrage Organization, and artist Norman Rockwell.

In 1934, Mr Baker's daughter, Mary,

sold the house to the Wildwood Civic Club for $6,000. The only alterations made were to remove a partition so that a larger meeting room could be formed. Later, the kitchen was remodeled so the space could be rented out for parties, weddings or other important family occasions.

Now this beautiful old home serves as the clubhouse for the Wildwood Civic Club who contribute the money they raise to award scholarships to local students. They also volunteer to help the sick, disabled

Leona Betz in sitting room she restored in memory of her husband George Buzz Betz, pictured with her above

and needy and in any way that will help the community and the nation. The group is part of the New Jersey State Federation of Women's Clubs.

The Friends of the J. Thompson Baker House organized in 1997 for the sole purpose of restoring the first historic home on the island. Groups and individual members have taken on a room to restore. Crest Savings, Carol Schoening, Pat Sorensen, Leona Betz and Sue Benner have restored six of the bedrooms.

Leona M. Catanoso Betz restored a bedroom and also decided to honor the memory of her husband George M. Betz by restoring a sitting room. Buzz, as everyone affectionately called George, graduated from Wildwood High an honor student and after his education at Duke University and four years of active duty in the United States Air Force, he returned to Wildwood to teach chemistry, physics and math in his alma mater.

He coached basketball and football and his teams played in many state tournaments. He taught at Wildwood High for 40 years, retiring in 1976. During the sum-

The bedroom in Wildwood Civic Club that Leona Betz restored

mers, he was the Director of Lifeguards in Wildwood Crest for 25 years.

When Buzz retired, Leona also retired as the Secretary of the Margaret Mace School after 40 years.

Leona and Buzz traveled and spent their winters in Florida. Buzz died in 2003 and Leona, who had been a member of the Wildwood Civic Club for 64 years, restored the sitting room in honor of George "for her love and the respect he's had throughout the community".

Included is a clock built by his great grandfather in Germany and a sewing box and a side table that Buzz made for his mother. Leona included some of their furniture that she reupholstered, along with an antique desk from their home.

Blueberry Buckle

Here is a recipe that Leona prepares whenever she is asked to bring a dessert to a pot luck or family occasion.

3/4 cup sugar
1/4 cup soft Crisco
1 egg
1/2 cup milk
2 cups sifted flour
2 teaspoons baking powder
1/2 teaspoon salt
1/2 teaspoon nutmeg
2 cups blueberries, washed and
    drained

CRUMB TOPPING
1/2 cup sugar
1/3 cup sifted flour
1/2 teaspoon cinnamon
1/4 cup soft butter

For the cake part, thoroughly mix the sugar, shortening, and egg. Stir in the milk. Sift together the flour, baking powder, salt and nutmeg. Stir into the egg mixture. Finally blend in the blueberries carefully. Spread the batter in a greased and floured 9-inch square pan.

To make the topping, mix together all the topping ingredients until crumbly and sprinkle over the top.

Bake in a moderate oven (350 degrees) for 45-50 minutes, or until a wooden pick thrust into center of the cake comes out clean.

Yields nine squares

Fox Park
One businessman's dream for a greener Wildwood

A ROMANCE beginning with a vacation at the beach doesn't always succeed, but it did for Betty Sacks. She was living in Brooklyn, NY, when she came to Wildwood on vacation in 1940 and met her future husband, Oliver Fox. "Ollie" was in business with his father in Fox Men's Wear on Montgomery and Pacific Avenues (across from the high school).

After their marriage, Ollie opened his own store in 1947 – Oliver Fox Men's Shop at Cedar and Pacific. Ollie played the trombone and was a member of the musicians' union. He was often called to play or fill in at the Starlight Ballroom. According to Betty, "In the Fifties and Sixties, Wildwood was the Las Vegas of the east coast." She met Liberace, Tony Bennett, Marty Allen, Damita Joe, and Charlie Spivak performing at clubs.

Betty is proud of the Fox family history in Wildwood. Edward Zelig Fox, her father-in-law, known as E.Z., had the foresight to begin the Wildwood park system.

Born in Latvia, E.Z. came to Holly Beach from Leeds, England in 1910 with his wife Bella (Betsy) and son Isadore. E.Z. and his brother Sol founded Fox Brothers Men's Store. As it turned out, Sol Fox married Bella's sister, Celia. While living in Wildwood, E.Z. and Betsy had three more children: son

Memory Lane was dedicated in 1956, another dream of E.Z Fox to have a tribute to those who lost their lives in service to the US; Betty Fox at the grand opening of the Doo Wop Experience in April 2007. Previous page: Fox Park Postcard (Wildwood Historical Society), and the refurbished Fox Park playground in 2008.

PARKS ESTABLISHED BY E.Z. FOX IN HIS LIFETIME

Cedar Park at Oak and Holly Beach Avenue, the Derbyshire building, was torn down at Twenty Sixth and Pacific for another park; in 1938 the William H. Bright Park at Glenwood and Pacific was dedicated. Then E.Z. began plans for a park at Poplar and New York Avenues. The Holly Beach School on Andrews Avenue was torn down and became a park. Bricks from the school building were used to build the flower beds, and flagstone from the school was used for walks. The original school bell was placed on metal from the old fire escape and the roof over the bell came from discarded blackboard slate. A plaque was placed on the school bell and dedicated to Henry Chalmers, a teacher and principal of the Holly Beach School. The original May pole is dedicated to Lanning Myers, the first Wildwood High School principal who became superintendent of schools.

Oliver and daughters, Lillian and Dorrit.

E.Z. loved the beach, "often setting up a tent and sleeping there overnight," says daughter-in-law Betty. His dream was for beautiful tree-lined and flower-filled parks for all to enjoy. During the depression, many property owners couldn't pay their taxes and the city foreclosed. E.Z. talked the city commissioners into reclaiming the properties for parks. He was appointed to the first Wildwood Park Commission in 1932, along with Edward Bradway, Louis Reber, John Keating and Thomas Delaney.

In 1933, Nick Silvidio was hired by the

Fox Men's Wear was on Pacific and Montgomery Avenue – above is Oliver Fox Men's Shop, which was on Cedar and Pacific, in Wildwood (Wildwood Historical Society)

Betty Fox's Noodle Kadoodle

This is a "wonderful recipe," says Betty which, when tried by a relative, was named Noodle Kadoodle. Betty suggests to "make two and freeze one."

10 oz medium egg noodles
2 oz butter, melted
1 cup sour cream
8 oz creamed cottage cheese
1/2 cup sugar
1 apple, diced (or 2 if you wish)
1/2 cup golden raisins
4 eggs, beaten
1/2 cup milk
3 cups cornflakes
1/2 stick butter or margarine, melted
1/2 teaspoon sugar
1/2 teaspoon cinnamon

Heat oven to 400 degrees. Cook the noodles and drain. In a bowl, combine 2 oz butter, sour cream, cottage cheese, sugar, diced apple, golden raisins, beaten eggs and milk. Add the noodles. Combine well and pour into a non stick sprayed 9 x 13 pan.

Top the noodle mixture with cornflakes, then drizzle with 1/2 cup melted butter. Combine sugar and cinnamon and sprinkle over cornflake topping.

Bake for 15 minutes at 400F. Then turn oven down to 350 and bake for an hour, until sides are brown.

Yields 12 servings

Park Commission to beautify the ends of the streets that meet the boardwalk. According to Betty Fox, "Nick's golden fingers" improved Wildwood. E.Z. was named Chairman of the Park Commission and suggested the city acquire the full block bounded by Montgomery, Atlantic, Ocean, and Davis for a park. Funds were collected by neighbors for planting trees and flowers and spreading topsoil, because E.Z. wanted the park to be built at no cost to the city. The park, now known as Fox Park, was dedicated on June 14, 1936.

When the tennis courts were completed and ready, those wishing to play were charged 25 cents an hour. Ball fields were planned and Memory Lane was dedicated in 1956, another dream of Mr Fox to have a tribute to those who lost their lives in service to the US. Recently Betty Fox and her family consented to use part of the park for the Doo Wop Experience and band shell.

Fox Park will always be for citizens and visitors since it has been designated as part of the Green Acres program by the state and can never be sold or used for housing. E.Z. Fox was a visionary and did as much as he could to beautify and provide recreation.

Green's Bike Rental

A free-wheeling family for five decades

I
F YOU vacation in Wildwood Crest, and you rent a bike, chances are you rented it at Green's Bike Rental. Morton and Pearl Green started the business more than 40 years ago, where it is still located near the corner of Ocean and Cresse Avenues. And it is still in the Green family, now owned by their children Jerry Green, Suzie Green Lombardo and Joan Green Cohen. Suzie Green Lombardo and her husband Jim are the proprietors of Suzie's Sweets and Gifts, a boardwalk store.

When Morton and Pearl Green were married in 1937 in Philadelphia, they didn't realize that 23 years later they would be in business in Wildwood Crest. They bought a restaurant at the corner of Ocean and Cresse, and called it the Green House. They ran it for 15 years, selling in 1975. It is now operating as The Seaside Diner.

Morton and Pearl began their bike rental business in 1963, next to the restaurant. When they sold the restaurant, they decided to keep Green's Bikes. In 1999, a new, two-story building was constructed on the site. Morton and Pearl's footprints are embedded in cement in the front of the bike rental building. In memory of Morton Green, a large clock has been mounted on the front of the building because Morton always wanted visitors to meet "under the clock at Green's".

When the bike rental business began, only simple balloon tire bikes with foot brakes were available to rent, but now there are mountain bikes, hand brakes, free baby seats, free helmets, side-by-side bikes, double bikes, choppers and surreys of all sizes.

Growing up in the summers, sisters Joan and Suzie and brother Jerry helped out

Opposite page: Looking south to Wildwood Crest around 1940. The largest building on the right was the Midway Motel and then just behind it, at Cresse and Ocean, the one story building later became the Green House Restaurant and Beach Grill. On the left you see the Wildwood Crest Fishing Pier. Brother Jerry Green, sisters Joan Green Cohen and Suzie Green Lombardo in front of Green's Bike Rental. This page: footprints of Morton and Pearl Green.

Pearl Green's Brisket

Pearl Green served this brisket recipe in the Green House Restaurant when it was operating and she always made it for family and friends in her home.

4 lb beef brisket
1 large onion, sliced
1 envelope onion soup powdered mix
2 lb potatoes, peeled and quartered
1 lb carrots, peeled and sliced
Garlic powder
Italian seasoning
Paprika
1 10 oz can cream of mushroom soup

Remove surface fat from brisket. Add onion to the bottom of a large pot or roasting pan. Place the brisket on top and cover with onion soup mix. Sprinkle meat with some garlic powder, Italian seasoning and paprika. Add water to the pan so it is filled halfway up with water - about 4 cups.

Cover pan with a lid and bake at 375F for two hours. Spread the mushroom soup over the meat. Add potatoes and carrots and cover the pot and continue baking about 2 more hours, or until fork-tender. The longer it is cooked, the better it tastes. (You may have to add more water.)

Remove meat and allow to cool. "Remember to cut against the grain", says Suzie, "so you will get a clean slice."

Yields 10-15 servings

Morton and Pearl by working at the bike rental business. When Pearl and Morton passed away in 1999, the three took over.

The siblings are aware of the changes that have been made since they have been operating the business at that corner. There were no motels between Green's Bikes and the beach when they started. The Aqua Beach Motel was one of the first built and it had eight rooms then. Now there are several huge motels in front of them, including the Aqua Beach Motel. And next to them the Siesta Motel stood for many years, but that was torn down in 2004 and is now a condominium complex. The Green family is happy that the area has been updated and that there is a new look to the Wildwoods.

Photo taken around 1997 of Morton and Pearl Green with two of their devoted bike renters - Gregory and Amy Sultner - who still stop by the shop

A photo of the Surf Inn on the right in 1950s, looking down Leaming Avenue. The Reef Inn is on the left. (Clunn family photo)

Surf Bikes
A hot dog purchase leads to a family legacy

IN 1945, Charles and Anne Jaggard came to Wildwood. Unhappy in Darby, Pennsylvania, they were invited to Wildwood by Anne's sister, Katherine Olwell, and her husband Joe, who owned Cromwell Hotel on 26th Street in North Wildwood. Charles stopped to get a hot dog at the custard and hot dog stand called the Surf Inn at the corner of Leaming and Ocean in Wildwood. The two women who owned the stand wanted to sell it and asked Charles if he was interested: $10,000. That was an extraordinary amount, especially since he only had $900 in the bank.

Anne convinced Charles to borrow the money, and it happened that the owner of Richman's ice cream heard that they were hoping to buy the concession and loaned them the money. The concession was selling Breyer's ice cream at the time, and after the deal went through they were soon selling Richman's!

The couple ran that concession for 40 years, with bathers lining up along the beach to buy, especially hot dogs. Their daughter Joanne and her husband George Minnitti decided to open a bike rental behind the concession and they called it Surf Bikes. When they opened it in 1962, a Schwin rented for 25 cents an hour.

The Jaggard family lived upstairs over the Surf Inn, also referred to as Jaggard's. Daughter Miriam remembers going down to the beach as a youngster and when she heard the national anthem playing over the loudspeaker she would come back to the Surf Inn because she knew her parents were closing up for the night. To make ends meet, Charlie drove an oil truck in winter.

Miriam Jaggard Clunn and her husband Frank bought out her sister and brother-in-law and took over the bike rental business. The original space occupied by the Surf Inn has been rented to the Surf Shop since 1981. Frank Clunn has since passed away and Miriam remains active in the business with the help of family and friends.

MIRIAM'S MEMORIES

Miriam was one year old when she came to Wildwood-by-the-Sea. In first grade at St Ann's School she remembers there were 90 kids in her class. "Can you imagine having to put 180 gloves on in the winter," says Miriam.

The school doctor was Dr Fath and he was also their family doctor. He gave as much time as needed to speak with and examine a patient. Miriam's mom didn't have enough money to pay for a visit to the doctor, especially in winter when the business was closed. Dr Fath said he would wait for his money until the summer.

Pictured above are clockwise from left: family friends Ed Doyle and Charlie Weber, Miriam Clunn, Michele Lowry (niece), Brook O'Donnell (granddaughter) and grandsons Brian O'Donnell and Bobby O'Donnell.

The Works

When the Surf Inn was in business and the bathers lined up for hot dogs, they would ask for "the works" on their steamed hot dog. Miriam and Joanne Jaggard mixed "the works" in gallon jars so it was ready to put on the hot dogs in the bun. "It was like a chow chow," says Miriam Clunn. "It didn't look so good," says Joe Saraco, who worked for the Jaggards in the Surf Inn for six years. He worked while he was in high school and lived with his grandparents over the summers down the Shore. Joe says, "Combining the ingredients might have saved a minute or two!" Miriam brought out the stainless bowls that they used then for the ingredients for topping the hot dogs. There were four bowls, one for mustard, one for onion, one for relish, and one for "the works."

3 tablespoons mustard (maybe more mustard, according to taste)
3 tablespoons sweet pickle relish
3 tablespoons dehydrated onions, presoaked and drained

Combine the ingredients and add to a jar. Cover and refrigerate. Serve on hot dogs in a bun.

Yields one cup

Anne Jaggard's Poor Man's Cake

Miriam Clunn remembers her mom's cake as delicious and called her older sister Joanne, who still has the recipe. Poor Man's Cake refers to the fact that there are no eggs, milk or butter in the recipe because during the war those ingredients were not easily available. The cake, made in a tube pan, tastes like a molasses cake but there is no molasses in it.

1 lb dark raisins
2 cups water
2 cups sugar
1 teaspoon salt
1 heaping teaspoon cinnamon
3/4 stick (6 tablespoons) oleo (margarine)
3 cups flour
1 heaping teaspoon baking soda

Combine the raisins, water, sugar, salt, cinnamon and oleo in a pot. Bring to a boil and stir well. Cool. (JoAnne remembers her mom cooled the mixture on the back porch in winter.)

Then add to the cooled mixture, the flour and the baking soda. Combine. Pour into a greased and floured tube pan. Bake at 350 degrees for an hour. Test with a toothpick to check if done.

Yields one cake (16 servings)

Crest Fishing Pier, Wildwood Crest, N. J.

Wildwood Crest Fishing Pier

The use has changed, but the pier still lies at the heart of the Crest

I N 1916, Philip P. Baker, the founder and first mayor of Wildwood Crest met with his friends to form a fishing club because of a "need by men of the community to enjoy good companionship and fishing." The men felt that fishing attracted families to buy a home in Wildwood Crest. This group of surf fishermen hoped for better facilities than those which they had. Turtle Gut, a stream which formerly cut across the island and separated Wildwood Crest from Two Mile Beach, was a favorite fishing spot for the founders of the club.

The Wildwood Crest Fishing Club incorporated in 1919, with Philip Baker as the first president. Meetings were held at the first clubhouse on Seaview Avenue. The meetings began with a Pledge of Allegiance to the flag, ended with a 50-50 drawing and, in between, cigars were smoked and business was discussed.

Mostly, the discussion centered around building a fishing pier, although in the beginning, they could fish out the back door of the fishing club. The water came up to Seaview Avenue in those days when Seaview was called Atlantic. As the water receded and the beach grew, Atlantic Avenue was moved out toward the ocean.

A fishing pier was built at Heather Road and the beach. Members who did not wish to fish enjoyed the ocean breezes in the clubhouse where they could also enjoy a friendly game of pinochle.

When the Fishing Club was active, there were rules. No drinking on the pier, a fee for guests, and no women were allowed on the pier past the yellow line. No one could fish if they were not a member or a guest. "No one off the street," says former member Mike Baklycki.

There was a blackboard on the site where the members would record fish caught, when, size, type, weight, and the fisherman. The fish caught was the important topic of conversation.

Mike Baklycki remembers that many fish were caught from the pier when he became a member in the late Sixties when he and his wife Mary moved to Wildwood

Inside the clubhouse on the Wildwood Crest Fishing Pier (Dave Callen); and men fishing on the pier (Wildwood Historical Society)
Opposite page: The new Wildwood Crest Beach Pier and, below, the old fishing pier clubhouse as it was (Theresa Williams)

Crest. He recalls that a blue shark measuring between four and five feet was landed and brought up on the pier. He remembers catching weakfish while fishing with his sons from the pier.

Ralph Catanese, who has lived in Wildwood Crest for about 40 years, remembers catching nine-inch-long Kingfish and other men caught bluefish, skate, striper, sea robin, blowfish, perch, spot, stingray, pilot, croaker and fluke. He remembered fishing from the pier at high tide in the year 2000.

Prizes were given for the largest edible fish each weekend in June, July and August, plus prizes for Monday to Friday and on July 4 and Labor Day. There was a Season Pool Prize for the largest edible fish caught from Memorial Day to Labor Day.

There was an Annual Casting Tournament and Pinochle Nights on Friday evenings in June, July and August. "A ladies night was held one Friday evening in August with prizes for the ladies," according to the 1954 Fishing Club yearbook.

Parts of the pier had to rebuilt when ice or a storm damaged parts of it. When the pier had to be extended in the early nineties, Mary Baklycki, got together with her friend Liz Pasquine, whose husband Lud (Ludwig) was also a member and the women decided to raise money by serving breakfasts and dinners. The first dinner was a Hawaiian Luau served in 1991 to a sold-out crowd – a Hawaiian group wearing hula skirts performed fire dances.

Because the beach increased in size, the pier was extended over the years. The

club members would raise the money, which might have been as much as $10,000 each, some even mortgaging their own properties. But finally the cost of adding on to the pier became astronomical; the end of it barely extended into the water during high tide, and the membership dwindled from the original 100. The pier was turned back to the borough of Wildwood Crest in 2006, not quite at the end of the 100-year lease.

Commissioner Don Cabrera got behind a renovation project completed in 2008 to make the pier compliant with Americans with Disabilities Act regulations. Now those with a handicap can observe the beach and ocean from an elevated and close-up view. Reopened as the Beach Pier, it has a new life and purpose.

Hawaiian Chicken

This recipe from Mary Baklycki was served at the first fishing pier Hawaiian dinner fund-raiser.

3 lb chicken, cut into parts
1 (16 oz) bottle Catalina Dressing
2 onions, thinly sliced
5 carrots, thinly sliced on the diagonal
   or shredded
4 stalks celery, cut on the diagonal
4 tablespoons pineapple preserves
Cooked rice

Place the cut-up chicken into a heavy pot and add water to cover. Bring to a boil, skim, lower heat and simmer, covered for about 20-30 minutes until cooked through.

Remove chicken from broth, saving broth for another use. Skin and take off bone and shred chicken.

Place the chicken in a large oven casserole dish with a lid. (Mary uses a baking bag). Cover with the Catalina dressing and wash out the dressing bottle with 1/2 cup of water and pour that over the chicken.

Then add the onions, carrots and celery. Combine well, cover and bake for 45 minutes or until carrots are tender.

Stir in the pineapple preserves and bake another 15 minutes.

Serve over cooked rice.

Yields six servings

In 1980, a plaque was placed at the bocce court in honor of Nick Silvidio, who receives the award from Commissioner Rich Nordelby. (Wildwood Historical Society)
Left: Players in 1980 at the new sign proclaiming Vincent Marsaro the manager. Left to right: Nick, Vincent Marsero, Sam Pantelone, Eddie (Marsero family)

Bocce in Wildwood
A fun game... taken very seriously

ANY night in the summer, walk down the boardwalk to Leaming Avenue and you will likely see a crowd of interested spectators looking down at the bocce courts from their boardwalk vantage point. While listening to Italian music, you can observe or play bocce on two courts that have been planned, developed and cared for by members of the Sons of Italy.

"They used to play for a nickel a game and fight over a nickel," says Dot Wadlinger, daughter of Vincent Marsero, a past manager of the bocce court. And Dot says, "They would take out a yardstick and measure the distance to see whose ball was closer to see which team gets the most points." Now the players use a TV antenna to check the distance between a loser and a winner. And one of the rules is now "no gambling."

Vincent Marsero was one of the group of men who brought bocce to Wildwood. He and some of his friends had established the Bocce League of America in 1935 in Philadelphia. When Vincent moved to Hildreth Avenue in 1970, he made a bocce court on Hildreth at the end of the street near the Boardwalk.

When the Ocean Towers planned to build in the mid-seventies, they needed that space so the bocce court would be destroyed. "It was a sandpit", says Vincent Marsero's daughter Nina, but the bocce players made a fuss and "held up construction of Ocean Towers".

It seems that the city owned several properties that were unused and the pur-

Angelo Verduci keeps score; Jeff, Craig and Terri Fitzgerald enjoy the pleasures of bocce by the beach

Terri Fitzgerald's Crab Dip

Terri Fitzgerald smiles when she says "my Italian grandfather, Luigi Bochese came here through Ellis Island... so that blood line entitles me to play bocce." Terri and her family learned how to play while they were in Wildwood during vacations. Now that women and children can also play, it is a great family activity. Terri's recipe may be halved and also served cold as a spread.

2 (8 oz) packages light cream cheese, softened
8 oz light sour cream
4 tablespoons light mayonnaise
2 teaspoons Old Bay seasoning
Juice of 1/2 lemon
2 teaspoons dry mustard
3 shakes garlic salt
1 lb special crab meat
1 cup shredded cheddar cheese
Paprika

Combine all ingredients except 1/2 cup of the shredded cheese and the paprika in a bowl. Place in an ovenproof 1 1/2-quart casserole dish. Top with extra cheddar cheese and paprika. Refrigerate until baking time. Bake at 325 degrees for 30 minutes. Serve hot with crackers. Refrigerate leftovers.

Yields six cups

pose was to turn them into parks. There was a piece of land at Leaming Avenue and the boardwalk which the city allowed the bocce players to use to build a court. The city still owns this piece of land.

Nick Silvidio was in charge of the parks until he retired in 1957 but he didn't really stop working or taking care of the parks. Vincent Marsaro and Nick Silvidio were the founding fathers of the Wildwood bocce according to family members. E. Troiano and Sons with Ernie Troiano Sr in charge, built the forms for the bocce courts and Nick Silvidio took charge of adding the sand to the courts.

Vincent and Nick and their bocce-playing friends took good care of the courts so they could enjoy the game and the camaraderie of the men. Women and children were not allowed to play in

Bocce
is played with four red and four green balls aimed at one smaller ball, the pallina. The person or team whose ball comes to rest closest to the pallina wins. To begin, a bag of small red and white balls is passed around for players to choose teams. To pick which team goes first, they throw out their fingers and count them.

the early days. There was, and still is, no alcohol, no gambling, no swearing and no arguing permitted: the same rules that are posted on the court. But now women can play and anyone under 12 can play accompanied by an adult.

Left: Stanley Szczur on the beach (Szczur family)
Above: Ben Bachman and his balloon tire rolling cart

The Fudgie Wudgie Man
On a sweltering day, such sweet and cool relief

"HERE Ya-R ice cream!" Memories of a day on the beach are not complete unless you hear the call of the ice cream man. An ice cream on a stick or a frozen fruit ice tastes so cool and refreshing when eaten on the beach. Ice-cold water is also a welcome treat on a hot day in Wildwood. (No water is sold on the North Wildwood beaches.) Only the Wildwood and North Wildwood beaches have ice cream vendors walking on the beach. In Wildwood Crest the hotel owners don't want competition for their coffee shop businesses.

The selling of ice cream began in 1971, with the vendor carrying a heavy insulated box on one shoulder strap. The box was filled with the Popsicle brand of frozen confections packed in dry ice. Now the sellers push a cart with balloon wheels up and down the beach.

There are only 15 licenses granted and these only to armed services veterans. A fudgie wudgie man has to retire for another vendor to fill his sandy shoes.

Joe Duncan, a North Wildwood councilman, has been on the beach almost 35 years. He carried a box for 20 years before he got wheels. Sandwiches and the Fudgesicle are the most popular confections except on hot days, when he sells more ices and gelato. "I'm the loudest guy on the beach," says Joe.

One of the other veteran ice cream vendors (he's been pushing a cart since 1991) is Vietnam vet Ben "Chip" Bachman, a Health and Physical Education teacher at Wildwood High. Other ice cream vendors known to natives and visitors by name are Roland Bevler and Bob Harkins. Pop Redding, now deceased, was another popular old-timer, working the beaches for 36 years, while Gus Kefalianos had been walking up and down the Wildwood beaches for

Councilman Joe Duncan enjoys meeting and greeting visitors on the North Wildwood beach

40 summers. You could find Gus sitting in his wheelchair at the end of the Convention Center ramp to the beach, selling ice-cold water. He died in 2009.

Stanley Szczur was a Fudgie Wudgie Man for 36 years when he retired in 1988. He remembers, "In the beginning the box weighed 80 or 90 lbs and was filled with about five items." He recalls "twin pops, Popsicles, Creamsicles, Fudgesicles, and ice cream sandwiches. Seven of the twin pops sold for one dollar in those days. Fathers would gather round and buy seven pops for their family!"

Stanley says now there are "too many varieties." It is hard to push all that on the beach, and it is such a long walk to the boardwalk to refill the cart. The prices have increased as well as the varieties: a Spider-man, Sponge Bob or Choco Taco frozen treat costs $2.50 and a bottle of water is $2.

After Stanley retired, he worked as a parking lot attendant at the Montgomery Avenue entrance to Wildwood Convention Hall. He enjoyed the job as much as he enjoyed his job as ice cream salesman. Not only did he get attention with the familiar "get your fudgie wudgies here," he also wrote a poem he would repeat as he walked by the ocean's edge. Stanley's son Philip has set the song to music and recorded it.

I am the man on the beach
Who the kids love to meet
I'm the fudgie wudgie man.

I walk through the sand all day
Pushing my cart all the way,
Shouting out all the sweets
That the kids love to eat.

Fudgie Wudgie Wudgie
Chippy Chippy Chipwich
Icy icy pops
Creamy creamy sicles
Hey diddle diddle
Ice cream in the middle
Choco choco; who wants a taco?

At the end of the day
When the crowd goes away
I take my cart
And go on my way
Waiting for a hot and sunny day!

Stanley Szczur©

Marge Szczur's Stuffed Cabbage

1 head cabbage
1/4 pound bacon
1 lb ground meat (3/4 beef, 1/4 pork)
1/2 cup rice, raw
Salt and pepper to taste
2 (6 oz) cans tomato paste
1/2 large onion, chopped (about 1 cup)

To steam cabbage, carve around the core but do not remove the core. Place in a large pot of water with the core down, bring to a boil, cover and cook until the leaves are softened – 20-30 minutes. Uncover, allow to cool.

Cook the bacon and save the fat. (Originally fatback was used, but since that is difficult to purchase now, "I use real fatty bacon," says Marge.) Pour bacon fat into a bowl. Cut bacon into small pieces and add to the bowl. Add meat, rice, salt, pepper, and mix.

Make sure the cabbage has cooled. Remove from the pot and drain. Take a leaf and put a spoonful of meat mixture at the core end and roll up. Repeat until all the meat mixture is gone. Save some of the outer leaves and put in bottom of a pot. Add filled cabbage. Put another saved leaf or two on top.

Add tomato paste with enough water to cover halfway up the pot. Top with onions. Cook for an hour on the stove then bake at 350F for an hour.

Yields 8-10 servings

Jake Bush, from Pine Hill, NJ brushes his teeth on the Sunday morning of a Beach Jam. Right: the Beach Jam is an impressive sight to behold (Morey Organization)

The Scouts Beach Jam
This mass gathering is a sight to behold

TWICE a year, in the spring and fall, Morey's Piers hosts a Scout Beach Jam. As far away as Canada in the north, North Carolina in the south and Kansas in the west, 8,000 boy and girl scouts, leaders and their families come to spend a weekend on the beach in Wildwood. When the tents are set up, it is an amazing sight.

For the spring Jam, during the third weekend in May, the scouts begin to arrive in Wildwood from Friday afternoon until ten or eleven at night. After they set up their tents on the beach at Morey's Piers between Schellenger and Spencer Avenues, they can go on the rides, walk the boardwalk or ride the tram. Many bring sandwiches or pack food for dinner since

Troop 19, St Catherine's of Sienna Parish in Wayne, PA. Back row: Jack Schittig, Gary Tchorzewski, Brian Schittig, Kevin Schneider, Jack Pierri, and Mark Vincent Front row: Bianca Schneider, Selena Schneider, Russell Schneider, Liam Vincent, Ryan Tchorzwski, Daniel Ferrer and John Modrzynski, assistant scout master.

there is no cooking allowed on the beach. Otherwise, there is plenty of food available on the boardwalk

For a reasonable fee of about $59 a person, they can camp on the beach for two nights, ride the attractions on Morey's Piers, and are served two breakfasts and a dinner on Saturday. Morey's allows them to use their bathroom facilities all night,

which includes the piers, rented porto-potties and restroom trailers.

On Saturday morning, breakfast is served from 6:30am until 10:30am. When the scouts get their meal tickets, they are assigned a time to get in line for breakfast, as you can imagine, feeding 8,000 people would need organization.

In the afternoon, Morey's Piers offers

a merit badge program in oceanography. In 2009, a badge in aviation was offered for the first time. The scouts are taken by bus to the naval air station for a tour.

Saturday night a meal is served to the scouts, usually consisting of their favorite foods: hot dogs, hamburgers, and maca-roni and cheese. The meals are set up at the end of Mariner's Landing Pier, where

Raisin, Oat and M&M Granola

Make this granola at home and bring it to the Beach Jam for an easy, nutritious and delicious snack.

2 1/2 cups old-fashioned or quick oats
1/2 cup sunflower seeds, unsalted
1/2 cup coconut, unsweetened (optional)
1/2 cup sliced almonds
1/4 cup water
2 tablespoons canola oil
1/4 cup honey
1/2 cup raisins
1/2 cup M&Ms or chocolate chips

Preheat the oven to 250 degrees. Spray a sheet pan with non-stick spray or oil the pan.

In a large bowl, combine the oats, sunflower seeds, coconut and almonds. In a separate small bowl combine the water, canola oil and honey. Pour over the oat mixture and stir.

Spread oat mixture over pan and bake for one hour. Stir every 15 minutes to mix in the toasted edges. Remove the pan from the oven when the mixture is golden and toasted. Cool.

When the mixture is cooled, stir in the raisins and M&Ms. Store in glass jars, plastic containers or plastic ziplock bags in the refrigerator. Will keep for several months.

Yields five cups

a catering facility is located. After dinner there is a bonfire on the beach.

A breakfast is served on Sunday and then it is time to pack up for the ride home. It is an immense undertaking and good weather is hoped for; but rain or shine, they are out there for three days having fun and enjoying camping on the beach.

"Morey's handles all the reservations", says Merideth Fiorucci, who is Executive Director of Events and Entertainment. She has been working for Morey's organization for more than 20 years and has been handling the Beach Jam since its inception, in 1985.

The Fall Beach Jam is a two-day event at the end of September, attracting about 4000 campers. "The fall event probably doesn't attract as many because it is close to the beginning of the school year when there are a lot of school activities," says Merideth. "Once the school year gets underway, the scouts can have fund raisers to raise money for the scouts to attend the Beach Jam in the spring."

Each year, more and more scouts camp on the beach for this ultimate experience.

Sentinels of the Shore

Wildwoods' lifeguards

THE safety of the beaches depends on the lifeguards: a good-looking group of young athletes who can swim, handle a lifeboat, patiently answer questions, and don't mind sitting on a chair, high over the water, from 10am-5:30pm every day.

In 1895, the hotel and bathhouse owners hired the first lifeguards in order to provide safety to bathers. In 1905, Wildwood took over the job – the first two public lifeguards were John Wick and Daniel Briggs, who earned $50 a month.

An article in the *Wildwood Leader* of June 1933 announced, "Two Women are Named to Wildwood Beach Patrol." Wildwood was the first city on the Atlantic Coast to employ women lifeguards. "The Wildwood Beach Patrol is offering... the rather unusual prospect of being rescued from the surf by a blonde – or, rather, by two blondes... Miss May Ottey, of Ardmore, PA and Miss Florence Newton, of Philadelphia are the two blondes."

Michael Potter, a Wildwood Beach

Opposite page: In 1933, Wildwood was the first beach patrol on the Atlantic coast to employ women. Above: the beach patrol in 1925. (Wildwood Historical Society)

Above: North Wildwood Beach Patrol guard Brian Musso, and two women in the 1930s (Wildwood Historical Society). Opposite: Lifeguard stand (Cape May County Department of Tourism)

Patrol (WBP) lifeguard in 1951, writes in the *Wildwood Leader* that he always wanted to be a lifeguard and he'd seen *Baywatch*. "Who wouldn't want a job that paid you to sit in the sun, swim in the ocean, and occasionally be a hero?"

He found that the vigorous training and schedule was more than he thought, but he got through it. He wrote: "Lifeguards are some of the funniest, craziest, and most likeable people you'll meet

anywhere. Lifeguards come in all different shapes and sizes, but they are all genuine, sincere, hardworking men and women doing a difficult job."

Nearly every lifeguard stand now has two guards – originally there was only one to a stand. And they had to drag the stand under the boardwalk because the water rose so high on the beach... many rescues were under the piers.

In the Sixties and earlier, flag sig-

nals were used between lifeguards. Today there are cell phones. The uniform changed from a one-piece tank suit in the Forties to a three-piece outfit in the Sixties: tank, shirt and trunks. The colors were always red and white. Today, the uniform is a blue bathing suit, a red tank top and a gray sweatsuit with red and blue WBP letters on each, a whistle and a lanyard. Officers wear a white tank top.

The fabric is wash-and-wear, usually polyester, and made to last through the summer. Wool was the fabric of choice in the first days of the beach patrol.

"A uniform gives recognition and professionalism," says Lou Cirelli, the chief of the lifeguards in Wildwood and also the President of the South Jersey Lifeguard Chiefs Association.

According to Lou, a retired guidance counselor from Woodrow Wilson High in Camden City, there are 70 lifeguards employed in the summer in Wildwood. Usually the same lifeguards are hired every summer but they lose about 12-14 every year and these have to be replaced.

In order to be hired as a lifeguard, the applicant has to pass certain requirements. First there is a 500-yard swim, which must be completed in 10 minutes or less, in a crawl stroke. This qualifies the person to continue. Next there is a mile run on the beach which the person must complete in 7 1/2 minutes or less. Then there is a run, swim in the ocean and run back to the starting point.

A dash into the surf to make sure the future lifeguard is comfortable in the ocean is next and finally a personal interview to make sure the person will fit into the organization, has the right attitude and is "coach able" says Lou Cirelli.

If the person qualifies, then there is an eight-day school where the rookies are taught rowing, rescue techniques,

Manuel Montero and Anthony Zuccarello at Sam's Pizza Palace, a lifeguards' favorite (Photo by Michael Hirsch)

CPR, first aid, and handling injuries and emergencies. Finally, the rookie is assigned a senior guard.

Competitions are held between the various city lifeguards. These competitions "are good for morale, good for social events and to bring the families together." The life guards of today "are better trained and the operation is more professional than in the past. More is

expected of lifeguards today," says Lou. "They are proud of what they do."

After the season is over, Lou Cirelli, who has been employed since 1965 by the Wildwood Beach Patrol, spends time repairing and replacing equipment. Some of the lifeguard boats are more than 30 years old but they are well-maintained and still used and safe.

Brian Musso, pictured in the life-

North Wildwood Beach Patrol guard T.J. Figaniak, from Perkasie, PA, spends the summers visiting his grandparents

Peanut Butter and Jelly Sandwich

When asked about a favorite food, most of the lifeguards mentioned peanut butter and jelly sandwiches. As Lou Cirelli says, it is "the good old American lunch. It keeps for hours in the lunch container, it doesn't need refrigeration and it is not expensive." Not that anyone needs a recipe, but here it is for posterity!

4 slices multigrain bread
1/4 cup creamy natural salt-free and
    sugar-free peanut butter (just
    ground peanuts)
1/4 cup strawberry preserves or
    grape jam

    Cover 2 of the slices of bread with peanut butter - more than 1/4 cup if desired. Cover with preserves or jam and then the second slice of bread. Cut in half to form triangles. Wrap with plastic wrap or place in a ziplock bag.

    Yields two sandwiches

guard chair on the Third Avenue Beach in North Wildwood, is a resident of Wildwood Crest. A lifeguard since 2004 and a sociology student at Atlantic County College, Brian works as much as he can past Labor Day since the lifeguards get time-and-a-half pay if they can stay on; an enticement to have lifeguards after school begins.

TJ Figaniak, from Perkasie, Pennsylvania, shared the chair with Brain Musso in 2006. TJ spends the summers visiting his grandparents, who have had a house for 30 years on Ninth Avenue in North Wildwood.

To relax after work, most of the lifeguards get together to enjoy each others company. You might find them at Sam's Pizza Palace on the boardwalk enjoying a slice.

Treading the Boards
The ultimate Wildwoods pastime

Rolling chairs coming off the Cedar Avenue ramp – it was 75 cents an hour to ride them (Wildwood Historical Society)

THE boardwalk in Wildwood-by-the-Sea stretches from the welcoming arch in North Wildwood at 16th Avenue, down to the end of Wildwood at Cresse Avenue, a distance of about two miles.

Also referred to as "the Boards" or "the Walk", some form of the boardwalk has been in Wildwood since 1899 when 150 yards of boards were laid directly on the sand at Atlantic Avenue near Oak. To go for a stroll at the turn of the century, men were dressed in suits and women wore long, full skirts.

The boards, which were taken up in the winter and stored, gave them the opportunity to enjoy a walk closer to the ocean. By the next year the boardwalk was moved

even closer to the ocean, extended, and made more permanent by building onto pilings laid between Oak and 26th Streets.

In 1919, Oliver Bright, who was a councilman for Holly Beach and later was elected a commissioner when Holly Beach and Wildwood consolidated, thought the boardwalk should be moved even closer to the ocean. When he brought it up to the property owners along the boardwalk, they were against it. So Oliver Bright hired a team of laborers, and under cover of darkness, moved the boardwalk closer to the ocean. Oliver was removed from office.

By 1921, a new boardwalk was built from Cedar Avenue to Montgomery and on what is now Atlantic Avenue. By 1925, as the beach continued to grow, a petition was filed to move the boardwalk out to Beach Avenue. This new Boardwalk was held up by precast concrete pilings rather than the old cedar pilings which became worm infested and rotted. The boardwalk itself was constructed of 60 foot spruce planks except for the roller chair paths. Only two years later the boardwalk was extended from Montgomery south to Cresse Avenue. And again in 1928, it was extended north to 16th Street by North Wildwood Mayor George Redding.

As it grew, the boardwalk became important for fun, food, and shopping. The first roller coaster was built in 1910. Games of chance multiplied. Soon the boardwalk promenade began to attract everything

Charlie Douglass in front of his famous shop in the winter of 1943 (Wildwood Historical Society)

from top hat and cane vaudeville acts to international stars. Cab Calloway and Duke Ellington played at Scully's Convention Hall between Spicer and Spencer. The Starlight Ballroom and Hunt's Plaza attracted Benny Goodman and Glenn Miller in the 1930s.

Fudge, taffy, and candy became an important part of the boardwalk. Everyone visiting wanted a sweet to eat and to take home.

One of the oldest fudge businesses,

Douglass Fudge, began in 1919. In 1922, Charlie Douglass had a pavilion built across from the store so hot and tired walkers could rest in the shade and stop and buy fudge. There are two Mallins Candies still on the boardwalk that were started in 1946 by Jimmy Mallin. In 1953, he brought a mechanical taffy pulling machine from England to the boardwalk.

Ice cream became a popular boardwalk food. Waffles and ice cream and rectangular topped cones that held a block of straw-

In 1919, Oliver Bright, a local councilman, had the boardwalk moved closer to the ocean under cover of dark, against the city's wishes. He was removed from office.

berry, chocolate and vanilla ice cream were cool treats. The 28 flavors of Howard Johnson's ice cream was a popular stop. Kohr's ice cream still has two shops on the Boardwalk.

A hot dog stand was opened in 1909 by Earl and Mabel Groff at Magnolia near the Boardwalk which later became Groff's Restaurant. The Zaberer brothers started out with hot dog concessions on the boardwalk. Their mother operated Zaberer's Holliday on the boardwalk with early bird specials and Sunday dinners. There were many fine restaurants on the boardwalk.

The odors of corn popping, peanuts roasting, sausage, hot dogs and peppers grilling, pizza and pretzels baking are irresistible. Taylor Pork Roll, Lime Rickey made with fresh-squeezed limes, and Funnel Cakes beckoned you to try them. Who hasn't purchased cotton candy when its sweetness is carried through the air?

Arcades and games of chance attract the strollers. Many remember stopping to watch the Pig Slide where bets were placed as to which pig would get down to the bottom of the slide first. There were machines in which you could put one or two cents and you could purchase a photo card of a movie star like Buster Crabbe or Johnny Weissmuller. In the Vistascope you would insert a penny and see a movie of shuffled cards: 10 cards dropped and displayed sequentially. Spin the numbered wheels and the winner received a food prize. You could win a prize by throwing a dart to break a balloon, or pick up a duck from the floating water and choose a winning number, or the Kentucky Derby Race at Bobby Dee's where the prizes were cigarettes or the shooting galleries with real .22 shots.

Other arcade games from which you would collect coins or tickets to win prizes were ski ball or fascination. Randy Senna owns Flippers Fascination, a game which was invented in the 1920s and debuted at the 1933 World's Fair. For twenty cents a game, rubber balls are tossed over a grid of 25 holes, with players hoping to be the first to get a line of balls like tic, tac, toe.

Several movie theatres were on the boardwalk. The Strand opened in 1947 between Pine and Maple. The Regent Theatre opened in 1915 at Lincoln and the Boardwalk by William Hunt. In the forties he renovated it and in 1946 he added air conditioning. The theatre could seat nearly 1500. When Mr Hunt died, in 1970, Marty Falk purchased the theatre and had it gutted and kept only the original marquee. He renamed it the Boardwalk Mall, which contained 30 stores and a food court.

A Vistascope was a well-known sight on the boardwalk; and Charlie Zaberer's hot dog stand was another boardwalk fixture (Wildwood Historical Society)

Piers were built to hold amusement rides. The four men who were responsible for the piers on the boardwalk were Joe Barnes (Fun Pier), Gil Ramagosa (Sportland Pier), George Coombs (Marine Pier and Mariner's Landing) and William Hunt and his sons Bud and Guy (Hunt's Pier). Bill and Will Morey founded Morey's Pier in 1969 with the opening of a giant slide. The Morey family began to purchase the three main piers, refurbish them and add more exciting rides and a water park

Shopping was more than T-shirt shops. There were family shoe stores, clothing and beach wear and gift shops. Charles' Shell

Shop and the Boardwalk Chapel were popular, along with a bowling alley, roller skating, Skilo, and skyline miniature golf. There was a bandstand for morning concerts.

During World War II, the boardwalk lights were dimmed at night to prevent German submarines from using the lighted coast to target the silhouettes of allied ships. The sides of the lights facing the ocean were painted black. Still eleven ships were sunk within sight of Cape May County.

Boards had to be replaced in 1973 and the wood purchased was from the inaugural seating stands for President Nixon in Washington, DC. About 30 to 40 trailer truck loads of lumber were brought to Wildwood. In 1976, the reviewing stand wood from President Carter's inaugura-

Funnel Cakes

This Pennsylvania Dutch treat is popular along the boardwalk. The name comes from the batter which drips into the hot oil from a funnel.

2 eggs
1 1/2 cups milk
2 tablespoons sugar
1/2 teaspoon salt
2 cups unbleached flour
1 teaspoon baking powder
3-4 cups cooking oil
6 tablespoons confectioners' sugar

Beat the eggs in a medium bowl. Add the milk and sugar and mix well. Combine the salt, flour and baking powder. Add this to the milk mixture. Beat with a whisk until smooth.

Add enough oil to an electric skillet so there is an inch in the pan. Heat the oil to 360F. Using a funnel with a 3/8 to half-inch hole, put your index finger over the bottom of the funnel, allowing the batter to run slowly into the hot oil. Slowly move the funnel in circles larger and larger to make a circular pattern. The cake will be about 8" in diameter when done.

Fry until golden brown on one side and turn and fry the other side. Remove the funnel cake to a paper towel-lined plate. Drain a few minutes.

Add sugar to a sifter or strainer and shake over the funnel cake.

Yields six funnel cakes

The four men who were instrumental in building piers and rides on the boardwalk: Joe Barnes (Fun Pier), Gil Ramagosa (Sportland Pier), George Coombs (Marine Pier, Mariner's Landing) and Guy Hunt (Hunt's Pier) (Wildwood Historical Society)

tion was purchased to redeck part of the boardwalk.

The most prosperous years for the boardwalk were the Fifties. The piers flourished and the rolling cars were replaced by the tram car. The Starlight Ballroom drew about 6000 teens weekly to the record hops. The public was looking for challenging rides and games. On the Marine Pier (between Cedar and Schellenger) they had a Caterpillar, Miniature Golf Course, Old Train, Fer-

ris Wheel and basketball. On Hunt's Pier there were various childrens rides, go carts, a smaller roller coaster and miniature car rides.

By the mid-Seventies, the economy was faltering. Wildwood was developing a reputation as a vacation spot for rowdy kids. Many businesses closed and were taken over by T-shirt shops and 99-cent stores. Changes have been made over the past few years to keep the boardwalk a vibrant destination.

Taffy, Fudge and Ice Cream

A trip to the boardwalk would not be complete without them

A HUGE part of seashore memories are food related. Walk the boardwalk and you are bombarded by the sights, tastes and smells of food. You are enticed into eating as you go. Fresh pizza as it emerges from the ovens, the warmth and sweetness of cinnamon wafts by as you approach the pretzel bakery, and the sizzle of sautéed onions and peppers waiting to be spread into an Italian roll allures you to buy. There is nothing so delicious as walking and eating from a bucket of French Fries

or caramel corn. Who hasn't enjoyed licking an ice cream cone as it drips over your hand as it melts while you are walking?

Cousin Jackie remembers the fresh waffle and ice cream sandwich. Aunt Maxine looked forward to the cone with the rectangular top in which a strawberry, chocolate and vanilla block was inserted and then coated with chocolate and topped with a maraschino cherry. Marilee always stops at DAIRY QUEEN for a Peanut Buster Parfait. A walk on the boardwalk after dinner for my husband means a stop at

KOHR'S for a chocolate and vanilla twist atop a cone. To quench his thirst, he looks for his favorite beverage, a lime rickey, made with lime juice, sugar and soda.

For most, a vacation in Wildwood, means buying some fudge or taffy to eat right away and then some extra to take home. Wildwood has many sweet shops that invite you in to try some of their creamy confections.

Wildwood is the home of DOUGLASS FUDGE, still family operated since 1919. It could be the oldest operating business still owned by the same family in the Wildwoods: "our 89th year in 2009". The distinct black Scottie dog mascot on the red plaid boxes and wrapping paper were chosen because of the Douglass' Scottish-Irish heritage. They sell fudge, saltwater taffy, chocolate covered saltwater taffy, chocolates, cream mint sticks, molasses paddles, caramel corn, butter crunch, almond bark and rum butter toffee. They make all candy on the premises except for the gummy bears, licorice and hard candy.

The pavilion across the boardwalk from the store was built in 1922, so tired walkers could sit and also stop to buy fudge. Charlie Douglass, his brother Joseph and his wife Minerva and their three children:

June, Charles, and Harvey began their taffy business on Cedar Avenue. June's daughter, Barbara Bradley Dugan, is the owner now working with her sons James Bradley Dugan and Jason Alexander Dugan, the fourth generation.

LAURA'S FUDGE is another Wildwood fudge business, just off the boardwalk and begun in 1926. They sell 16 flavors of fudge and other tasty candies including candy that looks like shells and sugar free confections. Lori and Dave Roach are the present owners.

HANKINS FUDGE is located off the Boardwalk on Pacific Avenue at the north end of the shopping street between Maple and Glenwood Avenues. In 1946, George and Mary Hankins began making fudge, dipping chocolate, and rolling fondant in the garage where they lived on Columbine Avenue in Wildwood Crest. In 1950 he moved his candy making and shop to Wildwood Avenue and the Boardwalk. He was there for 10 years and then moved to Baker Avenue and finally to Pacific where the shop still operates.

George decided he wanted to retire and move to Florida. At this time, Tony Gorbatow, who had lived in Millville and spent his summers working in Wildwood at the games of chance and selling waffles and ice cream, was getting his haircut at Pete's and he heard that George Hankins was looking for a buyer of his fudge business. Tony, who until this time, was thinking of becoming a lawyer, decided to go home and talk about the business that was being sold to his twin brother Ken who had a degree in Food Science Management. So they decided to buy the business in 1976 and they are very happy that they did. George Hankins taught Tony and Ken how to make taffy as he learned it working at Fralingers in Atlantic City. Their time is divided so that Tony is there during the day and Ken takes the evening shift. "Ken is the manufacturer," says Tony, pictured opposite.

MALLIN'S FUDGE has two shops on the Boardwalk which were started in 1946 by James "Jimmy" Mallin who sold the shops in 1972 to the Silver family. They sold in 1977, to Joseph Dilks, who still makes all the varieties of fudge and also the one inch wrapped taffy. In the window of one of the shops stands the original taffy-pulling machine (pictured), which was imported from England in 1953 and is still used.

The ORIGINAL FUDGE KITCHEN, which has several shops on the Wildwood boardwalk, was opened in 1972 by brothers Joe and Paul Bogle. It is open all year if you get hungry for one of 20 different kinds of fudge in the winter months. Pictured right, offering samples, is Rhoda Phillips.

JAMES SALTWATER TAFFY is on the boardwalk. They sell fudge, but they are more famous for their large variety of salt water taffy. You can still buy the blue and white barrel packed with your favorite flavors of taffy.

Vegetarian Chili

Because Hankins Fudge partner Tony Gorbatow is a vegetarian, he enjoys making and eating a chili that contains no animal products.

2 tablespoons olive oil
1 cup chopped onions
3 cloves garlic, minced
1 cup shredded or finely chopped
    carrot
1 cup chopped celery
1/2 cup chopped green pepper
2 tablespoons chili powder
1 teaspoon ground cumin
1/2 teaspoon ground allspice
1/4 teaspoon black pepper
4 cups or 28 oz can tomatoes in
    purée or tomatoes diced in juice
2 cans (14.5 oz) dark red kidney beans
    (or 4 cups cooked beans)
2 cups cooked Jersey corn, cut off the
    cob or frozen corn
Cooked brown rice
Hot pepper sauce

Heat the oil in a large pot. Add the onion, garlic, carrot and celery and sauté for 5 minutes, until celery is softened. Add the green pepper, chili powder, cumin, allspice, and black pepper and mix. Add tomatoes. Bring to a boil, lower heat, cook for 20 minutes

Add the beans and corn and heat through. Serve on cooked brown rice. Pass the hot pepper sauce.

Yields 10 cups

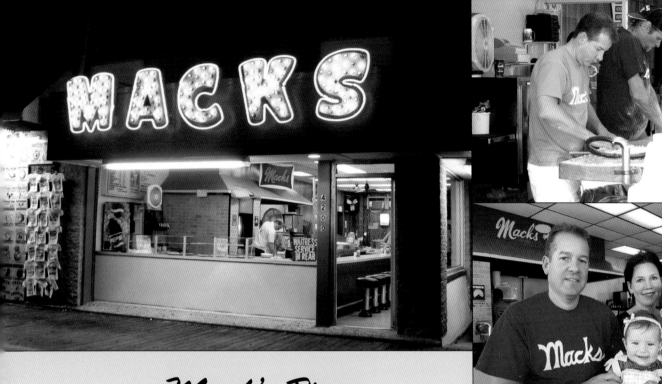

Mack's Pizza
An irresistible slice of boardwalk lore

AROUND 1950, Anthony and Lena Macaroni started a tomato pie shop in Trenton and later moved to Seaside Heights. In 1953, they moved to Wildwood and opened a Mack's on the boardwalk. At one time, there were four Mack's pizza shops in Wildwood, and now there are two. It's still a family-owned business

– the partners are Anthony's sons, Joe and Dominick (Duke), and Duke's sons, Darryl and Ron. Anthony became partners with a cousin, Vince Manco, and they opened pizza shops in Ocean City called Mack and Manco's.

In the Fifties, one could buy a whole pizza pie for $2.14. Each slice, served on a napkin then, was 29 cents.

A member of the third generation, Darryl Mack can usually be found in the Mack's Pizza nearest to the Wildwood Convention Hall on the boardwalk near Roberts Avenue. The tomato sauce is pumped up from the basement refrigeration unit through a clear plastic tube and spread directly on each pizza.

The second Mack's Pizza shop, on the

Mrs T. (Rose Tata) and the pink steps going up to the second floor at the Wildwood Avenue and Boardwalk business.
Opposite page: Darryl Mack with his wife Mary and their kids, Eoin and Laura. (Photo by Michael Hirsch)

Creamed Cucumber Slices

When I asked Darryl about a recipe for this book, he said "I don't have any recipes," and Mrs T. said she doesn't have recipes. Darryl eats a lot of pizza during working hours and he takes dough home and makes pizza at home but he says it doesn't taste the same as in the shop. "The ovens are the secret."

This recipe is an Irish recipe from Mary Mack's heritage.

1 large cucumber, peeled and sliced
1/2 red onion, thinly sliced
1/2 cup plain yogurt or light sour
    cream
2 tablespoons apple cider vinegar
1 teaspoon sugar
1 tablespoon chopped fresh dill or
    1 1/2 teaspoons dried dill

Combine all ingredients in a bowl. Mix well. Cover and refrigerate at least an hour before serving.

Yields four to six servings

boardwalk at Wildwood Avenue, is the one that many recall fondly. Pizza and Pennsylvania Dutch Birch Beer are the most-ordered combination and the preferred seats are up the pink steps to the second floor to sit at a table by the window with a view of the boardwalk, beach and ocean.

Rose Tata – or Mrs T. – can be found checking over the smooth running of the Wildwood Avenue shop on the "walk" as she refers to the boardwalk. Mrs T. had a business in Wildwood and when she closed it, Duke Mack convinced her to come work for him, which was more than 35 years ago. She was 89 years old in 2009, still a gem, fun to talk to, and with an amazing and contagious energy.

Watch the Tram Car, Please

The history behind those famous people-carriers... and THAT voice

IF YOU have been to Wildwood and walked on the boardwalk, then you have heard the familiar warning: "W-w-w-watch the tram car, Please!"

The tram car has been active on the Wildwood and North Wildwood Boardwalks since June 11, 1949, when Sebastian Ramagosa started the business. He had purchased some trams cars that were used at the 1939 New York World's Fair and 10 years later, he decided to use them as boardwalk transportation. The first drivers were uniformed women. He also employed a "starter," who had to make sure that the cars departed regularly so they wouldn't run too close together.

Eventually, Sebastian's son Gilbert and his wife Suzanne took over the business. Sue's good friend Marian Sandman, 85 years old in 2009, still lives in Wildwood and still sells tickets at the boardwalk tram car office.

The Boardwalk Special Improvement District Management Corporation, known as SID, now operates the tram cars. It is a private non-profit business, which not only operates the cars but also sees that the boardwalk is maintained and cleaned. It also provides family entertainment on the boardwalk – the SID pays the cities of Wildwood and North Wildwood to run the trams.

General Manager of the Tram Car Division is Kevin Lare, from West Cape May. Kevin explains that a 36-volt battery, which measures approximately three foot square and is located in the first car, runs the vehicles. One battery when charged can operate for eight hours, then a "changeover process" begins. The car has to go back to the garage to be charged and another comes out.

Right now the SID owns eight cars

Sue Ramagosa's Peach Ice Cream Pie

Sue says that light peaches, diet Jell-O or diet Cool Whip can be used to cut calories.

9-inch baked pie shell
1 (14-15 oz) can sliced peaches in juice
1 package of lemon Jell-O
1 pint vanilla ice cream
Whipped heavy cream or Cool Whip

Drain the sliced peaches, saving the juice. Measure the juice and add water to make it 1 cup. Bring the cup of juice to a boil. Take the juice off the burner and add the Jell-O. Stir until dissolved. Add half-cup of cold water and 1 pint of vanilla ice cream. Stir until the ice cream is melted.

Spread the drained peaches in the baked pie shell. Pour the Jell-O mixture over the peaches. Place in the refrigerator 4 to 6 hours before serving time. Cover with whipped cream or Cool Whip. Serve.

Yields one pie (about six to eight servings)

Marian Sandman, in the tram car office on the Wildwood boardwalk. Opposite page: An ad announcing the arrival of the new cars. (Wildwood Historical Society)

but replacements are needed. The original manufacturing company is no longer in existence, though a California firm has promised to make a new tram to the specifications of the SIDs. The one problem in making this tram is that it has to be able to make a U-turn at the Wildwood end of the boardwalk, where it is only 28 feet wide. This turn is "remarkable," according to Kevin Lare, "for a four-car tram."

Each car can carry 15 people with a capacity of 60 for each tram. Ride on the tram in the front car, just behind the driver, and you will wonder how the cars can get safely through the sea of people walking on the boardwalk. You will understand why the driver needs to sound the famous announcement "Watch the tram car, please!"

The voice for the recording is that of Floss Stingel. In 1970, she was asked to tape the warning message as a favor to her boyfriend, who worked for the Ramagosa family. Floss, who was not paid for the taping, still lives in North Wildwood and has become a celebrity – she is often stopped and asked for her autograph.

Carlson's FISH MARKE

OFFICIAL

WILDWOOD

Doing th

Central Avenue. By 1928, there were six more American stores in the Wildwoods: 17th and New Jersey Avenues, 3403 Pacific, 3921 Pacific, 4616 Pacific at Andrews, Park Boulevard at Montgomery and one at the corner of New Jersey and Sweet Briar Road in Wildwood Crest.

As the population grew, the American stores expanded throughout the towns and changed their name to Acme. There was a store where Fireside Pizza is now at 4101 Pacific at Youngs, and one at 3011 Pacific at Maple which had a huge neon sign that lit up the night. That Acme closed in the Sixties. It is now the site of Atilis Gym.

On June 14, 1956, a new Acme opened at Park Boulevard between Hildreth and Bennett Avenues. This store was state-of-the-art at that time. It was air-conditioned and it contained Magic Carpet doors: they opened by themselves as someone approached!

Since traveling by car was heavily promoted in the Fifties, the store was built so patrons could drive there. It had a large parking lot and you could drive up to the door and load your packages into the car.

By 2005, that Acme, the only one

Doo Wop Acme

How a famous old store got the Wildwood do-over

SMALL corner markets are always a part of a shore town, a place to find fresh produce, baked goods and breads, meats and cold cuts, sandwiches, newspapers or cleaning supplies. In 1904, there were many of these markets in the Wildwoods. A few mentioned by residents were the Ewan Meat Market on Pacific, Kammers Bakery, S.J. Coombs Market, and Baker Brothers Provisions; the last one closed in 1937. Another popular market was Fulginiti's Grocery which was across the street from the present Rio Grande liquor store at New Jersey and Rio Grande.

The coming of the railroads to Wildwood and the building of the railroad stations brought businesses to the area of the stations. The first American store was built in North Wildwood in 1903 at First and

Employees of the Acme on 3009 Pacific Avenue in 1943 were, left to right: unidentified, Anne Iaconangelo Zook, manager Marvin "Slim" Morton, unidentified, and Marion Shivers Mouklas. (David Williams) Below: Acme ad from the 1940s

Ted Kammer is a retired Acme employee. He retired after 39 years with the company. Theresa Williams worked for Acme for 15 years before retiring.

ACME MARKET: 3919 Pacific Avenue

Spencer and Pacific Avenues   WILDWOOD, N. J.

THESE SAME PRICES EFFECTIVE UNTIL OUR NEXT ADV.

Shoulders of Pork 18c lb

RUMP STEAK	
ROUND STEAK	
COUNTRY SAUSAGE	**28c lb**
HALF SMOKES	
RIB ROAST	
PIN BONE	
CHUCK ROAST *And we have plenty of it this week*	
BONELESS POT ROAST	**19c Pound**
HAMBURG STEAK	
SKIN BACK HAM	
STEWING BEEF	
STEWING LAMB	**12½c lb**
TAYLOR'S SCRAPPLE	
FRESH LIVER	

remaining in the Wildwoods, was no longer adequate to serve the population. The air-conditioning system needed to be replaced and the floor was no longer level. The big complaint of customers was that you would stop to grab something from the shelf and your cart would keep moving. Consumers wanted a larger take-out department and a larger fresh produce department.

So this Acme was demolished and rebuilt and opened on May 25, 2006 with a Doo Wop theme. The light blue paint, the original style signage, the neon sign and the art deco waves were included to give it the genuine look. The new Acme is double the size of the old one to accommodate the summer visitors as well as provide the residents with all the services they requested.

The Acme is now part of a growing list of buildings in Wildwood-by-the-Sea with a Doo Wop theme: others include TD Bank, Wawa, Walgreens and Harley-Davidson.

Theresa William's Olive Oil And Herb Dip

Theresa Williams retired from the Acme after working there about 15 years. Whenever her family comes for dinner, they hope she will serve this "bread dip". Theresa and her husband David have 27 grandchildren and three great-grandchildren at last count.

She uses the Acme multi-grain long rolls which she warms in the oven for about 10 minutes at 450F and then slices into about 8 slices each. She also uses some of the dip to sauté zucchini.

1 bunch cilantro, rinsed and trimmed
1 bunch parsley, rinsed and trimmed
2 cloves garlic, cleaned and sliced
1/2 red onion, sliced
Juice of 2 lemons
Juice of 2 limes
1 cup virgin olive oil

Add the cilantro, parsley, garlic and onion to a blender and pulse, stirring frequently until all is finely chopped. Add the lemon and lime juice and blend again. Finally, add the oil and blend again. Serve with sliced warmed French baguettes.

Any leftover dip can be refrigerated and then brought to room temperature to serve.

Yields about one-and-a-half cups

The new Doo Wop Acme on New Jersey Avenue and Bennett, and its expanded fresh produce section

Owner/partner Rick Hoff with his sons Cody and Garrett, and Jorge Delgado. Opposite: Carl (Loady) Carlson with a winning drumfish, his aunt, Esther Carlson Haun, and Beth Carlson (Porky and Mary's daughter)

Top: James Beaman in the truck and Dock Street co-owner Warren White. Above: original Union Fish Market.

Dock Street Seafood

Different families... same fresh ideals!

DOCK Street Seafood, at Park Boulevard and Otten's Harbor, began as the Union Fish Market by a group of Swedish men. In 1958, John Carlson and his wife, Clara, came to Wildwood, purchased the market and changed the name to Carlson's. John and Clara settled in Wildwood and expanded the business. They purchased the ice cream store next to it, converted it to a seafood take-out, and lived above it. John had a clam boat, named the *Elizabeth C*, and whatever he caught that could be used for bait he sold and delivered to county marinas.

John and Clara had two sons – John, who was nicknamed "Porky," and Carl, or "Loady". Porky and Loady took over the business when their parents retired.

Porky married Mary McBride, a Wildwood High graduate, who went on to work at the fish market as a book-keeper or in the take-out seafood department with her mother-in-law Clara. Mary says, "My mother-in-law was the cook, not me."

In 1985, when Porky and Loady retired, they sold the business to Rick Hoff and Warren White, who had worked for the Carlsons since they were kids.

Rick and Warren changed the name to Dock Street Seafood. Rick hopes his sons, Cody and Garrett, will continue the business.

Mom Mom Carlson's Deviled Crab Cakes

Grandmom Clara Carlson prepared the crab cakes for take-out at Carlson's.

1 lb can lump or backfin crab meat
12 tablespoons butter
3/4 cups unbleached flour
1 cup milk
1 teaspoon lemon juice
1 tablespoon sherry
1 tablespoon Worcestershire Sauce
2 teaspoons dried parsley
1 teaspoon dry mustard
1/2 teaspoon onion salt or powder
1/2 teaspoon garlic salt or powder
Salt and pepper to taste
1 tablespoon mayonnaise
Cracker meal
Beaten egg
Breadcrumbs

Melt butter in pan. Add flour and stir until combined. While still on low heat, add milk slowly, stirring until well combined. Add lemon juice, sherry, Worcestershire and stir well. Add parsley, mustard, onion salt, garlic salt, salt and pepper. Continue stirring and heating until thick. Remove from heat and pour over crabmeat. Add mayonnaise and stir until well combined.

Refrigerate, then shape into cakes. Dip in cracker meal, egg, then breadcrumbs. Pan or deep fry until brown.
Yields 10 (3 oz) cakes

Richard Bonelli, an artist who fell into the family business, sets up a produce display. Inset: the store as it looks today, and how it was in 1960. (Wildwood Historical Society)

Bonnelli's Market

Exquisite food prepared by true culinary artists!

B ONELLI'S Market has been serving customers at Spencer and Pacific since 1940. If you need a newspaper, a quart of milk, an apple, one tomato, some fresh Jersey corn, a made-to-order hoagie, or a roasted barbequed chicken for dinner, you will find it at Bonelli's.

Early in the morning, before the store opens at 7:00am, Richard Bonelli is in the store, accepting food deliveries. He then prepares his displays of fresh produce and meats, checks the shelves and begins his daily schedule.

Richard graduated from Wildwood High and Lafayette College in 1963 after which his original intent was a career in the arts, maybe even acting. But his father, who owned the market, became ill and died in 1969 and left the business to his son. You can see Richard's creativity in the artistic displays and also the food art on the walls, which he painted in 1994.

Richard's father, John Bonelli, also graduated from Wildwood High, in 1929. A year later, he opened a butcher shop next to the corner on Pacific Avenue, just across the street from the present market. His family, all the way back to the Middle Ages, were meat-cutters in Formia, Italy. In 1933, John moved his shop to the corner.

By 1936, John wanted to expand again. Just across the street had been an A&P which was vacated, so John moved across the street and, in 1940, turned the spot into a state-of-the-art grocery. "It was a pioneer market in its day," says Richard. The ad that appeared in the *Wildwood Leader*

Richard Bonelli still lives in the house where he grew up: a lovely old Victorian home only a block from the market

Sautéed Shad Roe with Turmeric

Jonathan loves to discuss recipes and he has a head full of them. When we were discussing which recipe to use here, he first suggested a Turkey Pot Pie and then went on to a stuffed fish with a bread stuffing. Finally, we decided to use this Sautéed Shad Roe since it was developed by Richard and Jonathan agreed that it is unique. Soft-shelled crab can be substituted for the shad roe.

1 set shad roe
1/2 cup finely-chopped onion
2 tablespoons olive oil
1/2 teaspoon turmeric
1/2 teaspoon cumin
Salt and pepper to taste

Heat the olive oil on medium high, add the onion, turmeric and cumin, stir and sauté until softened. Add the shad. Saute several minutes on one side until the shad is golden and then turn and sauté the other side until golden and cooked through.

Move the shad on to a plate and cut into bite-size chunks. Serve on toast points, cover with some onion and serve as an appetizer.

Yields four to six servings

announcing the opening of Bonelli's Market advertised eggs at 33 cents a dozen and steak at 59 cents a pound. "Compared to today's prices," says Richard, "that means if steak is $8.39 a pound, then eggs should be about $4.67 a dozen."

Richard's son Jonathan, also a graduate of Wildwood High and of culinary school, has joined the business and is responsible for all the sandwiches and any of the take-out foods prepared behind the counter. He cooks all the beef, pork and chicken to his standards. He roasts the turkey breasts and bakes the ham. He has built a thriving lunch business. The *Newark Star Ledger* in 2000 named the hoagies at Bonelli's the tops in New Jersey.

While you are waiting in line for your take-out food, you will notice classical music playing in the background – unless there is a Phillies game being played! The conversation of those in line usually centers around the quality of the food and how often they come to Bonelli's. A Bonelli business has been continuously operated in Wildwood for almost 80 years.

While you are waiting in line and reading over the list of hoagies, give the Formia hoagie a try: garlic, thinly-sliced rosemary grilled pork (or sausage or chicken), imported provolone slices and broccoli rabe, sautéed in olive oil and garlic, and served on a hoagie roll. Delicious!

Says Richard, "To me, the perfect customer is someone who comes in and orders an Old World Hoagie… and let us do it."

Dewey Wallpaper and Paint, now the site of Ambiance Hair Salon. Opposite: Cartolano sisters – center Carol and from top right, clockwise, Mary, Ann, Josephine and Natalie (Nettie)

Dewey Wallpaper and Paint
Memories of nights around the juke box

AT THE corner of Bennett and Pacific Avenues, where the Ambiance Hair Salon is now located, sat W. F. Carof and Sons Paints, founded in 1937. The original owner was Wolf Carof and then his son Max Carof took over and made it a grocery store for a short time.

In 1946, the Cartolano, Donofrio and Capelle families moved to Wildwood from Wilmington, Delaware and took over the property, and it became Dewey Wallpaper and Paint. The partnership consisted of three brothers-in-law and their wives: Dominek "Dim" and Mary Cartolano, John "Dewey" and Sue Donofrio, and S. Paul and Molly Cappelle. Dewey and Sue left the partnership and moved back to Wilmington and when they left, Dim became known as Dewey. The remaining two brothers-in-law, Dim (Dewey) and S. Paul kept their partnership and enlarged it by purchasing houses and a business on the boardwalk. The brothers-in-law sold the paint store in the early Sixties, when it became a flower shop.

The Cartolano family lived in a four-bedroom bungalow, just behind Dewey Wallpaper and Paint with their five daughters: Josephine, Mary, Natalie, Ann and Carol.

Josephine Cartolano Daning remembers that there was only one phone for the home and business. When there was a call, the phone rang in the shop and also in the house. During work hours the phone was answered in the paint store, but there was a signal that meant the call was for the girls and they should pick up the phone.

When the girls were in high school, they received so many calls that a separate phone line was installed for the house.

Their dad, Dewey, was also a paper-hanger so when he was out doing a job, the girls had to mind the store. Josephine remembers that all of the sisters hated that. They would sit on the paint cans and wait for customers or phone calls.

Growing up in a shore resort meant that, in the winter, there were only a few occupied houses on the block but in the summer, there were more kids around. Summer meant looking forward to seeing familiar families and their children who came back every year and stayed all summer. Summers were fun and busy. Playing in each other's yards and enjoying summer activities together was special.

Josephine remembers several girls would all go to the beach, come home, shower and dress for dinner. And they did really "dress" says Josephine: "Pretty, fancy dresses."

Winters, in the early grammar school days, Josephine went roller skating at Wildwood Rec (Wildwood Recreation Center) at Rio Grande near Locke's Ice Cream, which was open year-round. Locke's Ice Cream was on Rio Grande and Pacific and "Mr Locke dipped the ice cream with his artificial hand."

Josephine has fond memories of her high school years at Wildwood Catholic. Every Friday night and Sunday afternoons

Today's Depot Market restaurant was previously Snuffy's, where the kids would dance around the jukebox

there were basketball games, both home and away, and the students attended all of them.

Weekends meant Saturday night dances at Crest Pier or hanging around the juke box at Snuffy's, at Astor and New Jersey, to tunes such as "In The Still of the Night" and "Johnny Be Good". Snuffy and Flo made the teens feel welcome. They made up a drink for the kids called "The Number" which they all ordered. Josephine thinks it was a combination of soda and chocolate syrup. After a date, especially a movie, the kids went to the Tom Cat, which opened late and stayed open all night.

SHOPPING IN THE FIFTIES

Josephine remembers all your shopping could be done on Pacific Avenue in the Fifties. For lingerie, they went to the Cotton Shop that later was called the Martha Shop. For children there was the Baby Shop or Tot Town. Shoes were purchased at Aldine's, Silen's, or Meyer's. For women's clothing there was Ruth Feld's or Moderne and for men there was Gidding's and Allen's. There were drug stores with soda fountains: Jackson's on Pacific and Fitzgerald's at Wildwood and Atlantic. For groceries, there was Bundschu on the first floor of a building at Pacific and Bennett. And there was Hughes Market, at Rio Grande and New Jersey.

Mom Mom Mary Cartolano's Homemades

For Thanksgiving, the Cartolano family still gathers in the family home in Wildwood to enjoy an Italian five-course meal: soup, antipasto, pasta, turkey and the trimmings, and desserts. The pasta is Mary Cartolano's "Homemades" recipe. It makes enough pasta for the 40 family members who attend!

5 lb unbleached flour (20 cups)
Salt
12 eggs
1 tablespoon oil
1/2 to 2 cups water

In a large bowl, make a well with the flour, minus a little to use while rolling out dough. Sprinkle salt over flour. In well, beat eggs, oil and about half a cup of water. Gradually pull flour into egg mixture until dough forms. Add water if necessary to make dough pliable. Knead well.

Let the dough rest for a while, then knead again before rolling out, using a pasta machine. Roll thin, about 1/8-inch thick. Cut into desired width for spaghetti, fettuccini or linguini.

Cook in boiling water until tender, about 6-9 minutes.

Yields about 40 servings

Top: The Tom Cat vehicle that was used in parades in Wildwood. Left: Tom Cat owner Tommy Taylor. Above: Silen's Department Store on Pacific Avenue has been in existence since 1919

Green's Liquor Store
Established after Prohibition, and still thriving today

GREEN'S Liquor Store received the first Wildwood liquor license given after prohibition in 1936. Irwin Green, or "Greeny," owned the store, on bustling Pacific Avenue, when Wildwood was a vibrant year-round community. The Aldene Apartment building at Cedar and Pacific was owned by Morris Green, Greeny's father. The store was on the first floor corner of the building.

When the commissioners decided to revitalize Pacific Avenue and change it into a mall, Greeny moved his store and formed a partnership with two lawyers: his nephew, Henry Gorelick, and John Groon. In 1972, the partners established Green's at its present location at Hildreth and Pacific, on property owned by Gorelick. In 1975,

Carl Groon, John's brother, became a partner. Carl is the working partner – you will find him in the Hildreth store. There is now a second Green's Liquor Store, at 26th and New Jersey Avenue. Greeny opted not to continue in the business and retired when "Greens Two" opened.

Carl feels lucky to grow up in Wildwood. "It is a great area in which to live, with all the beneficial characteristics of small-town America: everyone knows each other and go from grade one to high school graduation together." Carl and his wife Donna Maiale Groon raised three children here.

Civic-minded and always working to improve the Wildwood community, Carl is the Mayor of Wildwood Crest.

Patti's Pound Cake

Patti Bottino is Donna Groon's cousin. Donna says, "Everyone in my family loves pound cake and this recipe seems to be the only one that bakes here at the shore without a line of batter left in the middle. We make it quite frequently."

2 1/2 cups sugar
3 1/2 sticks butter
5 eggs
1/2 teaspoon vanilla
1/2 teaspoon lemon extract
3 cups flour
1 teaspoon baking powder
1/2 teaspoon salt
1 cup evaporated milk (or 1/2 cup milk)

Preheat oven temperature to 350 degrees. Grease and flour an angel food, turks head or bundt pan.

Cream sugar and butter with electric mixer. Add eggs one at a time. Add vanilla and lemon extract. Blend. Add all other ingredients. Blend with electric mixer for 5 minutes on high speed. (Leave shield on if you have an electric stand mixer.)

Fill pan with batter. Bake for 80 minutes on center rack to prevent burning.

Cool and remove cake.

Yields one pound cake

Top: the Aldene Apartment building at Cedar and Pacific was owned by Morris Green – Green's Liquors was located on the first-floor corner; and the store as it is today, on Hildreth and Pacific. Opposite page: Green's Liquor Store in 1960 on bustling Pacific Avenue; Mayor Carl Groon received the Peter Holcombe Memorial Community Service Award in 2008 for his public service spirit and tireless efforts to improve the Wildwood island community (Photo by Gil Trejos)

Fams Furniture Store

Tracing the lineage of a famous family store

VIOLA and Antonio Bilotti, hard-working Italians, moved to Wildwood from the Philadelphia suburb of Upper Darby/Clifton Heights in 1947. They opened a furniture and appliance store on Pacific Avenue in 1948 which began as a branch of the Philadelphia furniture and appliance store, Porrecca and Santini. The

Bilottis moved the store into the old Grassi Building on 4401 Pacific. In 1958 they moved again, to 103 E. Baker Avenue, calling it P&S Furniture, named for their daughters Phyllis and Susan Bilotti. In the Fifties, the motels were just starting to take off and the Bilottis found that furnishing motels was a good business.

During the motel building boom, any

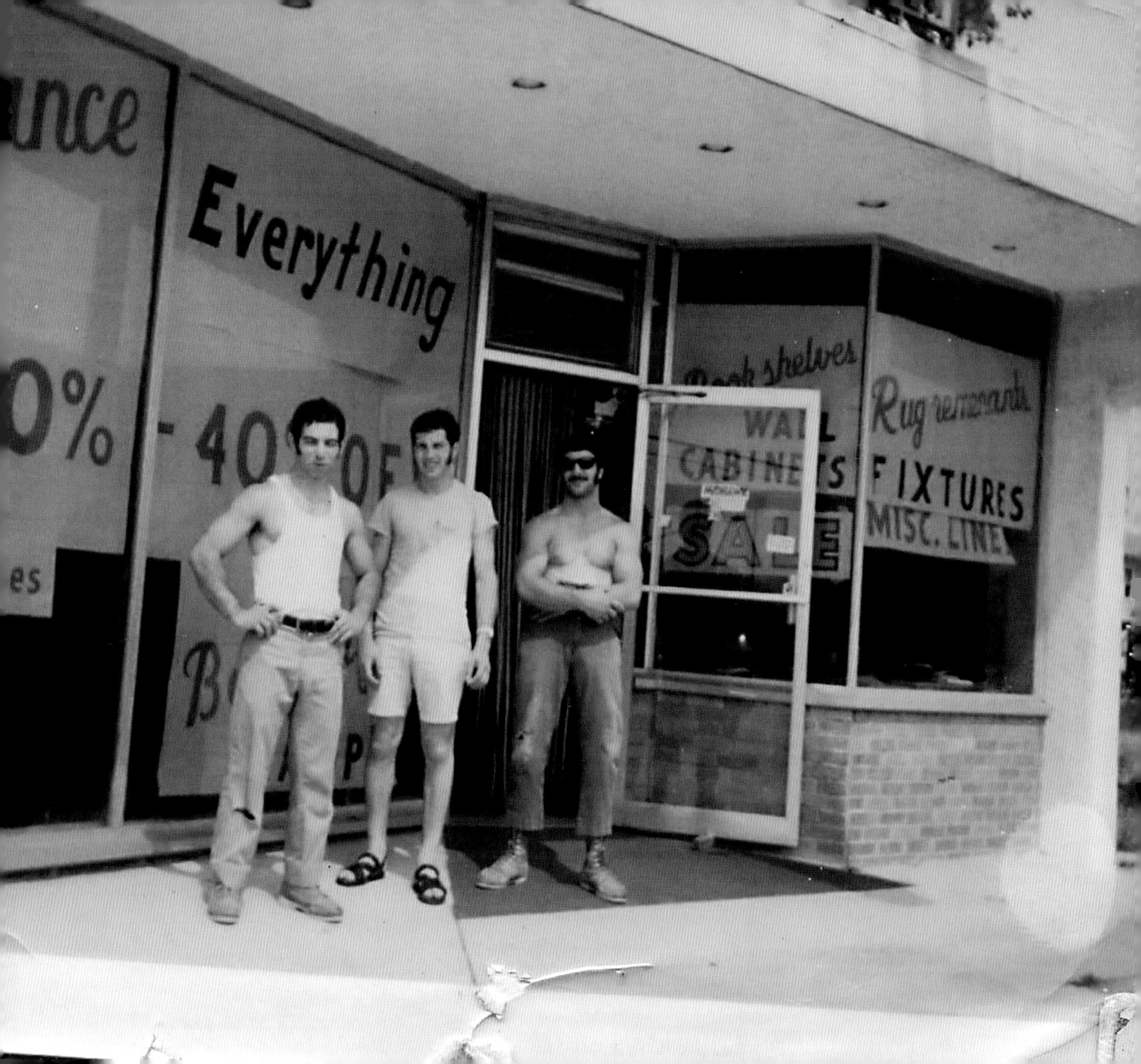
Everything
Rug remnants
FIXTURES
MISC. LINE
SALE

CRUISING UP PACIFIC AND HANGING OUT AT THE TOM CAT

PHYLLIS Bilotti Bethel enjoys reminiscing about growing up in Wildwood and her high school days, which includes hanging out at the Tom Cat, on Rio Grande. After a snack there, she and her friends would get in their cars and just "cruise" up Rio Grande to Pacific and ride north on Pacific to 26th Street.

Pacific Avenue was filled with shops in the Fifties. Murphy's and Woolworth's were popular for shopping or eating at their luncheonette counters that were filled with locals all year round. Sol's Dress Shop, Fox Brothers, Giddings, Silen's and Brown Jeweler's were just a few of the other popular shops.

Food was purchased at the Acme, seafood at Carlson's, now Dock Street, and for Italian produce and groceries, her mom shopped at Flacco's, which was owned by friends of her parents.

Her aunt, Elizabeth Russo, owned the popular restaurant on Park Boulevard called Russo's Gingham Club.

Silen's, Brown Jeweler's, and the Acme are still open.

Top: Phyllis Bilotti Bethel on her porch enjoying the company of one of her six grandchildren, Jamie Peters. Above: Phyllis lives in this house which her father moved from a beachfront property around 1950

Viola and Antonio Bilotti opened P&S Furniture in the early Fifties

small houses that were close to the beach were torn down or they could be purchased and moved. Antonio bought several vacant lots in Wildwood Crest and then moved two of those beach cottages to his lots.

In those days, a house could be moved, a foundation built and electrical and plumbing installed for $6500. So Antonio moved one to a property on West Morning Glory and one to West Buttercup. Phyllis Bilotti Bethel lives in the house on Morning Glory.

Antonio and Viola not only operated the furniture and appliance business but also a cot and crib rental business and the Wildwood Travel Agency.

By 1968, the Bilottis were ready to retire and Anthony "Tony" Antonelli and

Owner Tony Antonelli in front of his FAMS P&S Furniture on Baker and New Jersey Avenues

Cubanelle Stuffed Peppers

Viola Bilotti was an excellent cook. She made pasta every night: Sunday and Thursdays were spaghetti and meatball nights. Phyllis, her daughter, says "other nights it was pasta and soup, pasta fazool, or pasta and peas." Viola put everything in her meatballs. There was no recipe - she didn't use them. But here is a recipe that comes close.

The cubanelle is a long narrow green sweet pepper, also referred to as an Italian frying pepper or Italianelle.

15 large or 20 small cubanelle peppers
3 cups plain breadcrumbs or day old
    bread cubes
3 cloves garlic, minced
Several sprigs fresh Italian parsley,
    chopped, or 1 1/2 tablespoons dried
1/2 teaspoon black pepper
1/2 cup canola oil
1 can anchovie fillets with oil, chopped

Remove stem end and seeds of peppers; wash and drain. Combine breadcrumbs, garlic, parsley, black pepper, canola oil, anchovies and oil. Stuff the peppers. Using low heat, brown peppers in a small amount of canola oil.

Lower the heat more and cover the pan to cook the inside of the peppers, about 30 minutes.

Yields eight servings as a side dish

his friends were looking for a business to buy. Tony worked for a carpet company and met the Bilottis when he came to Wildwood to install carpet. A partnership was formed with his friends from Delaware County and they decided to call the store FAMS P&S Furniture and Flooring, a name formed from the first initials of the partners: Frank DiIoia, Anthony Antonelli, Michael DiIoia, and Sonny Vigilante. Now Tony is the sole owner of the business.

Left: Marie and Lou Flacco behind the counter in Flacco's. Above: Domenica and Antonio Flacco, the parents and store founders. Opposite: Anthony and Barbara Ann Flacco in the grocery aisle

Flacco's

Remembering 60 years of great food and special service

FLACCO'S Italian-American Grocery and Produce Market, better known simply as Flacco's, opened in 1941, when Antonio and Domenica Flacco moved to Wildwood from Philadelphia with their three children, Jean, Louis and Anthony. Their first market was in the middle of the block, so in 1960 a new and larger store was opened, on the southeast corner of Baker and Park Boulevard.

An article in the newspaper announced the opening of the new Flacco's with a ribbon cutting ceremony by Mayor Ralph Janos of Wildwood. The new store contained the "most up-to-date" equipment including a 14-foot food case, a 12-foot dairy case, a seven-foot ice cream cabinet and 22 feet of refrigerated produce counter.

The specials that were highlighted in the 1960 opening were: coffee at 59 cents a pound, ice cream at 89 cents a half gallon, bananas at 10 cents a pound, and sirloin, T-bone and porterhouse steaks at 79 cents a pound!

The most popular items in Flacco's were the sharp provolone, the Italian rolls and bread, the chipsteak meat, and the grated Romano cheese. They also sold eggs, freshly killed-poultry, milk and other dairy products at unbeatable prices. Lou's homemade Italian sausage – especially the hot sausage – was a favorite.

Lou was usually the designated driver to take a truck to the Philadelphia markets and bring back produce to the Jersey Shore, which they sold wholesale to restaurants in Cape May, Wildwood, Woodbine, Stone Harbor, Avalon and Sea Isle.

After their parents died, Dominica in 1989 and Antonio in 1990, brothers Louis

and Anthony remained partners and active in the business until 2005, when they closed the business.

Lou and Tony made many friends over the years. Their devotion to the community by their support was well known, especially the churches and the sports teams, in particular the Wildwood Warriors.

The Flacco brothers made special deliveries at no charge – for example, if an elderly person or one of their customers were sick, they would pack up the order and deliver it personally. Now that they are retired, they will count their blessings for the more than 60 years of business in Wildwood.

Marie Flacco's Gravy

While on vacation in Wildwood with several of her friends from West Orange, New Jersey, Marie met Louis Flacco at Vinnie's Luncheonette, behind the old Surf Club. They continued to write and call after that first meeting and eventually married.

Marie makes a "very easy and simple gravy," she says. Lou brought the meat from the market, and the meatballs are made without breadcrumbs or bread. Marie looked to Lou for the information on the ratio of ground beef and pork that he brought home for her to use in the gravy. Lou "loves the pork cooked in the gravy."

3 large (35 oz) cans plum tomatoes
3 cans (6 oz) tomato paste
Salt and garlic powder to taste
4-5 sprigs of fresh basil
4 tablespoons chopped parsley
1 lb Lou's sweet Italian sausage
1 lb end cut of pork loin
2 lb ground meat (pork and beef)
1 egg
2 tablespoons dried parsley or 1/3 cup minced fresh Italian parsley
3-4 tablespoons shredded Pecorino Romano cheese
Salt to taste

Place the tomatoes in the blender, blend quickly and add that to a large pot with tomato paste. Fill the paste cans with water to rinse them and add that to the pot. Rinse the tomato cans with some water and add that. Add salt, garlic powder, fresh basil and parsley. Heat on low, uncovered while preparing meat.

In a sauté pan, with some olive oil added, brown the sausage and the whole pork loin chunk. Add to the sauce as they are browned.

Place ground meat in a bowl and add egg, parsley, shredded cheese and salt to taste. Mix well and form the mixture into 12 large meatballs. Brown in the same sauté pan or bake in the oven on a baking sheet until browned. Place browned meatballs in the tomatoes, cover and cook for 3-4 hours. (Marie does not add any of the fat left in the sauté pan into the sauce.)

The gravy is cooking at the right temperature if there are little bubbles in the center of the pot.

Needless to say, the sauce is great over pasta or macaroni. Sprinkle with more shredded Pecorino Romano cheese.

Refrigerate or freeze any extra: it will taste even better the next day.

Yields four quarts

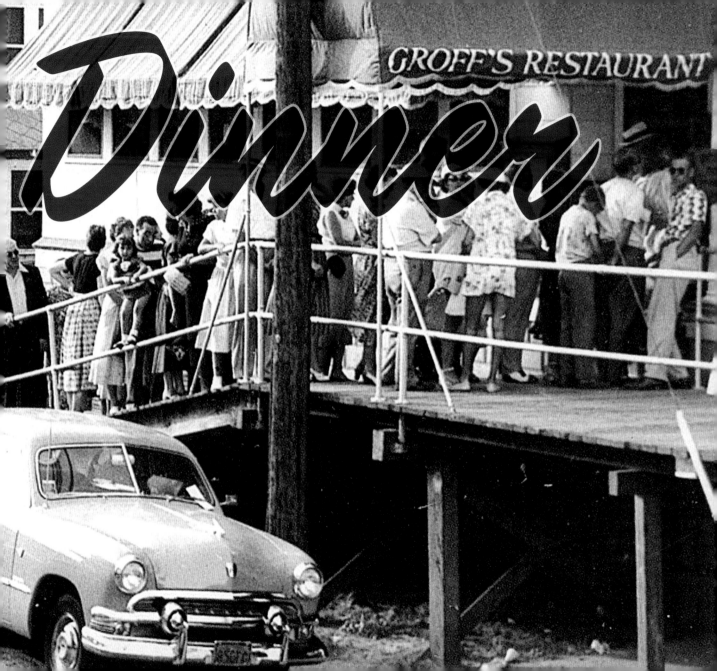

Captain's Table

A shark out front, and great memories inside

I N 1955, John and Phyllis Curcio DeFrancesco moved from Vineland, New Jersey, to Wildwood Crest where her family spent their summers. John formed a business partnership with his brother-in-laws: Frank Curcio and Lou Morey, husband to Ellen Curcio. In the late Fifties and early Sixties, Wildwood Crest had few buildings and these three brother-in-laws helped to build the town. They eventually each formed their own businesses with John

building motels such as the Compass, the Golden Crest, the Diamond Crest and the Crusader. Frank's specialty became single family homes and Lou Morey designed and built many of the now called "Doo Wop" buildings, for example, the Satellite Motel, the Chateau Bleu Motel, and the Surfside Restaurant.

John DeFrancesco and Lou Morey decided to buy the beachfront property bounded by Hollywood, Topeka, and Ocean Avenues and build a restau-

rant there. Lou designed the building to resemble a ship and the Captain's Table opened in 1963. It was "in the middle of nowhere and the only ocean front restaurant" according to Jana DeFrancesco Belansen, a daughter of John and Phyllis DeFrancesco. To attract patrons in the early days, Jana remembers, "a clown was hired to hand out coupons to tourists as they entered Wildwood on Rio Grande Avenue."

Eventually John and Phyllis became the sole owners of the Captain's Table. Mrs D., as Phyllis was called, ran the front of the house where she hired, was the bookkeeper, menu planner and food critic. John ran the back of the house and hired the cooks and kitchen help. Phyllis had graduated as a Home Economics major from Chestnut Hill College and she was a great cook, "not only Italian recipes" says her daughter Jana. Phyllis's mom, Antoinette Curcio, was a gourmet French cook.

The children worked at the "Table" as part of their growing up. Little Louie Morey and Little Johnny DeFrancesco worked as breakfast cooks. Jana said she "started in the business as a junior hostess, working under Hilda Weiner, who

FUN PEOPLE AT THE TABLE...

Jana DeFrancesco, pictured, right, a former owner of the Captain's Table, has wonderful memories of summer employees. Colin Whipkey, known as "Whip", was breakfast manager in the 1980s and worked under Ross Edwards, a dinner manager for 10 years. Ross had been a waiter and he married Marty Shields, who had been a waitress. Ross worked in the summers and in the winter months he was a schoolteacher and became an administrator in Millville, NJ.

Jana also mentions Ricky Grubb of Philadelphia, who came to work for her in the early 1970s and was "one of the best busboys". He later became a doctor... "a fine person," says Jana.

Another employee that Jana singled out was hostess Adele Hunter, a cousin from Wildwood who was a part-time school nurse and substitute in the Cape May County school system. She also mentions Marian Young, mom of Kevin Young, a local architect, and Annie King, who was a waitress and cashier and is now a doctor. Courtney Hornsby was another waitress, as well as Doreen Corino, who is now a lawyer and Wildwood Crest solicitor. Joe O'Neal was a manager fondly remembered.

Matthew Pressinger is fascinated by the fish tank in the restaurant. Opposite: The wooden shark sign that sat out front for more than 40 years (David Williams archives)

got her experience at Zaberer's. Hilda whipped me into shape!" Jana worked at the restaurant until her first child was born in August 1979, and then she turned her job of managing the restaurant over to her brother John. Sister Gail learned the financial end of the business from her mom. Gail worked in the office as banker and also would work as a waitress in an emergency. Later she kept the books at the Crusader Motel, another family enterprise.

According to John, "More than 10,000 students worked in the restaurant in the summer months during the almost 40

Mrs D'S Easter Pie

Jana DeFrancesco Belansen considers her mom's recipe box a treasure, with all her handwritten recipes arranged according to the holidays. In the Easter section, Jana found this favorite. Mrs D prepared her own crusts using Crisco, flour, eggs and water but here, the dough used is purchased refrigerated piecrust.

"The ham should be cut into tiny squares," says Jana.

2-crust pie dough
4 eggs, save 1 yolk to brush the top
8 oz ooked ham or pepperoni, finely
    chopped
2 hard cooked eggs, peeled, chopped
2/3 cup cooked rice
1 cup ricotta cheese
4 teaspoons Italian grated Romano
Salt and pepper to taste
A little milk to moisten if necessary

Grease or spray a 9-inch pie plate. Line the pie pan with one crust. Heat the oven to 350 degrees. Saving one yolk to brush the top crust, beat the three eggs and one white. Add the ham or pepperoni, hard-cooked egg, rice, ricotta cheese, Romano, salt and pepper and a little milk to moisten. Pour that into the pie shell.

Cover the pie with a top crust and flute edges. Brush with saved beaten yolk. Bake for 35 minutes until top is golden. Cool a little, and then serve.

Yields one pie (eight to 12 servings)

---

years of operation." Many romances were begun at the Captain's Table that were continued after the season ended – and many resulted in marriage.

Jana says in the early days, to hire the summer staff, they would interview college students who were given a two-week training course and were rated. The best ones were on the dinner crew, the second best were on the breakfast crew (that was when a full breakfast was served) and then the remaining were the lunch crew. The lunch was the easiest since it was mostly sandwiches and hamburgers.

On a busy night at the restaurant, there wasn't room for the line-up of diners to wait inside, so the podium was placed outside and the hostess took orders right there outside the door. There were three levels of dining: one with the stone floor and then two more with carpeted floors.

No matter where you sat, you had a great view of the ocean. In the last few years of operation, Jimmy Smithy, a local magician, would visit tables and perform tricks for the diners during the "Magic Hour".

John Jr was in charge until the restaurant was sold in 2002 to an investment group. It was demolished in 2005.

Duffinetti's
Goodbye to a dear old friend

DUFFINETTI'S was located in Wildwood Crest on New Jersey Avenue between Myrtle and Primrose. It closed in 2005 and was demolished.

When Duffinetti's closed, Trish Asselta was the owner. A restaurant had been in her family for 58 years. It was in 1947 that Duffy and Mary Asselta opened the Garden State Restaurant at Davis and Pacific in Wildwood. After 12 years, they moved to Taylor and Pacific. Then in 1963, they established Duffy's on the Lake in Wildwood Crest with cousins John and Phyllis DeFran-

cesco. When they sold that, they opened Asselta's Italian Villa at Heather and New Jersey and another in the Pan American Motel in Wildwood Crest. Then in 1965, they opened Duffinetti's, a new building on New Jersey Avenue. In 1978, they sold it to their daughter Trish, who operated it with help from her daughter Allison McNicholas, son David Asselta and granddaughter Madison Rose McNicholas.

Duffinetti's was known for great Italian food, especially the Chicken Florentine, the Veal Marsala and the Italian Combination of Ravioli, Cavatelli, Linguine, Stuffed

Shell and Two Meatballs. All the dinners were served family-style with a salad bowl, Baked Idaho, Sweet Potato, French Fries or a side of Linguine and Fresh Italian Bread with their special Pesto Dip. So many guests asked for the Pesto Dip recipe that the Asseltas bottled it and still sell it.

In the winter, when the restaurant was closed, it opened as the Sleepy Hollow Learning Center, a nursery school for children three to five years old.

Employees of the Asseltas returned year after year. John Salmieri, a cook for Duffinetti's, met his wife, Rosemary when she worked as a waitress. The last year the restaurant was opened, Rosemary was the salad person and made the apple pie, and their daughter, Marisa was a waitress.

Trish Asselta felt the last summer was

Opposiste: the famous Pesto Dip sauce; waitress Marisa Salmieri; and above, Mary and Duffy Asselta, the founders of Duffinetti's

"a very emotional one for me as it was very hard to say goodbye to folks I looked forward to seeing every summer. Some are fourth generation customers.

"My parents always taught me that it was important to make folks feel welcomed and comfortable, just like they were in my home. They all have truly become our extended family. When they would open the door to Duffinetti's, it was like Thanksgiving. You know, saying hello to relatives you haven't seen all year long and thrilled that they were able to spend time with you.

"Well, I take with me many years of wonderful memories and some good friendships."

Duffinetti's Italian Tilapia

Trish Asselta explained that everything served in the restaurant had some of the following crumb mixture on it. She thought that was the secret to a lot of dishes, making them unique. This crumb mixture, which she calls "Our Stuff," went into everything served at Duffinetti's. It might be used for flavor, for thickening, or for a topping for a broiled dish or vegetables, or if anything came out too soupy.

"Our stuff would absorb the liquid. So first you have to have the crumbs or our stuff always available," says Trish.

OUR STUFF

1/2 loaf day-old bread, such as Italian or
    a crusty bread
1 clove minced fresh garlic
1/2 cup grated Pecorino Romano
Salt and pepper to taste
1 1/2 teaspoons fresh chopped parsley
1 1/2 teaspoons fresh chopped basil
3 tablespoons olive oil

Grate the loaf of bread in the food processor until crumbs form. Pour into a large bowl; there will be about five cups. Add the garlic and mix it with your hands until it is all distributed among the bread crumbs.

Add the cheese, salt, pepper, parsley and basil. Mix well. Then drizzle the olive oil over the crumbs to moisten. Mix with your hands and place in a plastic bag. Keep refrigerated or it can be frozen and added to a recipe when preparing.

Yields five cups

ITALIAN TILAPIA

In the restaurant, an 8 oz portion was served per person. Raw spinach or slightly-cooked asparagus can also be added around the fish before baking.

8 oz tilapia or flounder fillet
White wine
Salt and pepper
1/2 cup fresh chopped Jersey tomatoes
Duffinetti crumbs (Our Stuff)
Shredded mozzarella cheese

Place the tilapia or flounder in a baking dish. Pour some white wine over the fish. Then cover the fish with the chopped tomatoes. Bake uncovered. Two to 3 minutes before the fish is done, sprinkle some crumbs on top and then over that some mozzarella cheese. Put the crumbs on the liquid, too. Then broil until cheese melts.

Yields two servings

Waitresses from Groff's in 1949 (Wildwood Historical Society) Right: The restaurant is still thriving today.

Groff's Restaurant
Eight decades of popularity, and it's as busy as ever!

A WELL-KNOWN and loved family restaurant close to the boardwalk and still operating, Groff's has been a destination since 1938 when it was established at the site by Earl M. Groff. It has remained family owned since then.

Earl came to Wildwood in 1918 from Reading, Pennsylvania. He rented a store and operated games, then in 1925, added a grill and sold hot dogs. Little by little he added more food items, especially Penn-

sylvania Dutch foods from his heritage.

Eventually he built and moved into the building that is still occupied by Groff's at Magnolia, near the boardwalk. Earl M. Groff retired in 1947 and passed ownership onto his two sons: Al and Paul. When Paul died in 1957, the business was maintained by Al and Paul's wife Dorothy.

Groff's Restaurant continued, always with lines to get in, and in 1970, the children of Al took over ownership: Dottie, Betty and Earl A. Groff. Since 1987, Earl

Above: Denise Shepherd and stepfather Earl A. Groff baking in the kitchen; Martha Groff, mother of Earl A. Groff. Opposite page: Kathleen Kelly, cashier, and waitress Brooke Bulifant in 2006; a view of the restaurant's interior.

A. and his wife Patricia and their children have been responsible for the continuation of Groff's.

Earl A. recalls that Groff's was the first restaurant in Wildwood to be air-conditioned. Before that diners were cooled by the large windows with screens and a huge ceiling fan. Groff's was also the first restaurant to purchase an electric ice machine. Previously they had ice delivered by the various ice companies in existence in Wildwood. The ice companies threatened Earl by saying they wouldn't deliver ice if their ice machine broke down. The machine worked for 20 years before it broke down and then Earl couldn't get ice because all the ice companies went out of business.

Groff's homey atmosphere, comfort food and fair prices are responsible for its popularity.

Entrées of meat, poultry and fish are served with a choice of three vegetables from a variety of choices daily, including Candied Sweets, Pepper Cabbage, and Cucumbers and Onions. Desserts, mainly pies, are a long-standing favorite, especially fruit pies.

Families enjoy a dinner at Groff's. "And that will continue", says stepdaughter Denise Shepherd, the manager, "we aren't going anywhere." Nice to know the legacy will continue.

Shoo-Fly Pie

Earl A. Groff took a handwritten copy of this recipe out of a locked drawer where he keeps treasured recipes from his mom, Martha Groff.

1 unbaked 8-inch pie crust shell

CRUMB MIXTURE
1 1/2 cups unbleached flour
1/2 cup packed light brown sugar
1/4 teaspoon salt
1/2 teaspoon cinnamon
1/2 teaspoon baking powder
1/8 teaspoon ginger
1/8 teaspoon nutmeg
4 tablespoons butter

Mix together until it looks crumb like. Set aside.

FILLING
1/2 cup boiling water
2/3 cup molasses
1/2 teaspoon baking soda
1/2 cup crumb mixture
Cinnamon

Preheat oven to 375 degrees. For filling, stir molasses and baking soda into boiling water. Add 1/2 cup crumb mixture and pour into pie crust shell. Sprinkle evenly with remaining crumbs and add some cinnamon.

Bake for 30 to 40 minutes until crust and crumbs are golden brown.

Yields one pie

Ravioli House

Pasta so good you could taste it for miles around!

ON THE corner of Bennett and New Jersey Avenues in Wildwood, you will find the Ravioli House, which has been in operation since 1970. They are famous for their homemade pasta and, on a summer night, you will find a line of hungry patrons waiting patiently outside, sitting on the benches or standing around talking. If you have never eaten there, you have probably had their ravioli, because ravioli and pasta prepared at the Ravioli House is sold and distributed to restaurants within a 150-mile radius of Wildwood.

Teresa and Antonio DeSanctis emigrated from Italy to Philadelphia as teenagers and met when they worked at a suit factory there. After they married they visited with Antonio's aunt, Esmeralda DiFonzo, who made pasta in a storefront of a building she owned at Bennett and New Jersey Avenue.

Eighty-year-old Esmeralda taught Teresa how to make pasta and since Teresa always wanted to own a restaurant, she was a good student. The DeSanctis family moved to Wildwood and purchased the building from Esmeralda.

With hard work, Tony and Teresa made a success of the business. Popular nightclub acts would stop by when appearing in Wildwood and taste the ravioli. Teresa and Antonio became good friends with Wayne Newton, Joe Pesci, Al Alberts and Julius LaRosa. Photos of their guests, including Tug McGraw, are framed on the walls of the Ravioli House.

In the Ravioli House kitchen with left to right: Uncle Vince DeSanctis, Teresa and Tony DeSanctis. Opposite page: Aunt Esmeralda and Teresa DeSanctis in front of the Ravioli House. (Wildwood Historical Society)

Teresa decided to open a pastry shop, which meant more hard work, but her children, Anna Marie and John, helped her as well as her two grandchildren, Joseph and Arianna Alosi. They gave her the incentive she needed to learn to bake the many Italian pastries. Now Teresa cares for her husband and works part-time as a baker and as a hostess at the Ravioli House. Daughter Anna Marie Alosi-Jakel and her husband Stephen Jakel take an active part in the business.

THE FEED FACTORY NEXT DOOR

The original building to the right of the Ravioli House was the C. W. Saul Hay and Feed business located conveniently near the railroad track. (Notice the top of the building.) It had been railroad property with a turntable in the days when New Jersey Avenue was called Holly Beach Avenue, built around 1900.

The Pennsylvania Railroad siding went right up to the warehouse and to the loading platform. It was the only railroad siding on the east side of the railroad in the City of Wildwood.

This building, which was owned by the DeSanctis family, was demolished and an addition will be built to increase the size of their commercial pasta business. At the time it was demolished, in 2008, it was a private residence.

Ravioli House Lemon Panna Cotta

1 package unflavored gelatin
1/2 cup warm water
1 quart heavy cream
Zest of 1/2 orange
Zest of 1/2 lemon
1/4 cup fresh lemon juice
1 cup granulated sugar
1 teaspoon vanilla extract

Dissolve gelatin in warm water in a small bowl. In a pot, add heavy cream with both zests, lemon juice, sugar and vanilla. Heat until sugar dissolves, do not boil.

Add in gelatin in water and mix well with a wire whip. Pour into individual serving cups. Refrigerate overnight. Top with whipped cream.

Yields eight servings

Another interior mural by Willard Berbow. Opposite: a fiberglas lobster in a pot on the roof

Schellenger's Restaurant
The greatest collection of seafood paraphernalia

CAN one more piece of sea memorabilia find its way to the roof of Schellenger's Restaurant? You must have wondered that if you passed the corner of Atlantic and Schellenger Avenues in Wildwood and noticed the brightly-colored seafaring paraphernalia on the rooftop.

In 1979, Valerie and Tony Trivelis and his sister Irene and her husband, John Karros, opened Schellenger's as a seafood restaurant. Before this, Irene and John owned restaurants in Philadelphia and summered in North Wildwood.

Irene and Tony's father, Demetrios Trivelis, was a shoemaker who emigrated to America from the town of Velvendo in Greece. A popular destination in the United States for Greeks from Velvendo was Cold Spring Village, New Jersey. Demetrios opened a shoemaker business in Cape May on Washington Street.

Before the restaurant became Schellenger's it was a steak spot called El Rancho. A chef preparing steaks in the window near the entrance occupied the corner. For several years, the previous owners operated it as a teen dance club, and when that was not successful they decided to sell. Irene and John Karros heard about the property, and came to have a look. They were hoping to move out of Philadelphia and this was a great opportunity.

Irene, John, Valerie and Tony became partners. Not only did they change the name of the restaurant, but the whole look of El Rancho. The six-foot-high windows in the front were removed, the entrance was changed to be closer to the center of the building, and a kitchen was built in the back.

In the early years, during the week Schellenger's was a destination for bus trips, which could bring in 600 hungry diners a night. A stage was built and every night two shows were featured, often with a comedian and a band to attract tours. Now, says Valerie Trivelis, "There are few bus tours. Seniors go on cruises or they have second-home destinations."

In 1990, Tony Trivelis began to add sea memorabilia to the restaurant. In the off-season, Tony and Valerie would drive up to Maine and then on the way home, they would take the road closest to the ocean and browse antique shops. Anything to do with the sea they would bring back, including old ship parts, miniature lighthouses, or boats. He had railings and small boat shacks built inside the restaurant. He bought collections of buoys. Inside there is a lobster sign from the demolished Captain's Table restaurant in Wildwood Crest.

The late Willard Berbow painted murals on the walls. First the walls were papered and then Willard covered the walls with his work. Mr Berbow also painted some murals in the Ravioli House.

Initially, Tony and Valerie's collectibles were added to the interior of Schellenger's, and then Tony got the idea to dress up the plain, flat roof. He put boats up there and had little houses built to hide the air conditioning units. Then he he heard about an artist who made fish out of fiberglass and he had him construct the huge lobster in the pot that occupies cen-

ter stage on the roof.

Chef Glenn Dunleavy has been working at Schellenger's for 20 years – previously he worked at Zaberer's, a well-known family restaurant in North Wildwood.

Alan Butler began tending bar in 2006. Before that, he used to bring bus tours to the restaurant for 14 years. He enjoyed visiting the restaurant and the opportunity of working there.

Several years ago a film crew came to Wildwood to make a movie called *The Shore*, starring Ben Gazzara and Leslie Ann Warren. Valerie remembers that a lot of the filming was done in Schellenger's and they fed the crew. The movie revolved around a restaurant and bar called the Hurricane, and the story of the waitresses and staff. Locals and actors were filmed at motels and on the beach with Wildwood lifeguards. "It was an exciting time," says Valerie, as she points to a photo taken with her and Ben Gazzara.

Schellenger's Lazy Man's Lobster

For those who like lobster and crab with no work, here is a 1 lb whole lobster hand picked and topped with 100% crab imperial.

1 whole 1 1/4lb lobster, steamed
1 (16 oz) can lump crabmeat
1/4 cup breadcrumbs
1 egg, beaten
1 tablespoon mayonnaise
1 teaspoon parsley flakes
1/2 teaspoon Old Bay seasoning
1/2 teaspoon salt
1/4 teaspoon mustard powder
1/8 teaspoon basil leaves, dried
1/8 teaspoon ground ginger
1/8 teaspoon ground black pepper
1/8 teaspoon ground red pepper or a
     dash of hot sauce
Dash of ground cloves
Seasoned breadcrumbs for topping

To assemble: pick and clean meat from lobster. Cut tail meat in half. Spray a small casserole dish with oil. Place all of the lobster meat into the casserole dish.

Gently combine remaining ingredients except the seasoned breadcrumbs and place on the lobster meat. Top with some breadcrumbs. Add a pat of butter on top. Bake at 350F for 15-20 minutes until bubbling.

Yields eight servings

Zaberer's

A wonderful world of eating in North Wildwood

BEGINNING in the late Fifties, Zaberer's was the restaurant that anyone driving anywhere near the Wildwoods had to visit at least once during a vacation – and, of course, the native "Woodies" enjoyed it much more than once! It stood at the north end of North Wildwood, on the road then known as Philadelphia Boulevard. It was a world all its own – a sign in front of the restaurant announced: "Welcome to Zaberville."

Frances Zaberer started the restaurant tradition in 1920 when she was the proprietor of a restaurant and hotel at 214-216 Glenwood Avenue called The Glenwood. Mrs Zaberer moved on to Hollidays, an old hotel which was on the boardwalk near the corner of Magnolia, a spot now occupied by Pierre's on the boardwalk. She had two sons, Charlie who was a sign painter and Ed who was a promoter, and they helped their mom run Hollidays. The boys also branched out and Ed had an ice cream shop

at Juniper and the Boardwalk, and by the 1930s each brother had a hot dog stand.

In 1955 the Zaberers bought and moved to the restaurant that was called El Dorado at the entrance to North Wildwood – it soon became Zaberer's Anglesea Inn. Brothers Charlie and Ed didn't get along and decided to separate. Charlie moved up to Atlantic City with his wife Rita, where he began a Zaberer's Restaurant on the Black Horse Pike near the Atlantic City Racetrack. Ed and his wife Ayne stayed in North Wildwood.

Zaberer's was a popular place... "Let's go to Zabe's." became practically a local catchphrase. The original restaurant seated 50 but it grew into a sprawling building and was renovated many times until there were eight dining rooms and four lounges and bars. There was a laundry facility on site, along with two full-time butchers and acres of free parking surrounding the restaurant.

There were hundreds of Tiffany original lamps inside and stained glass windows, especially in the Harvest Room, which was named after the stained glass harvest scenes in the glass along the wall. There were old theatrical posters, a barber chair, and an Atlantic City rolling chair. The rooms were packed with memorabilia.

WELCOME TO *The Wonderful World* of

ED ZABERER'S

WILDWOOD, NEW JERSEY

- HOME OF ZABERIZED COCKTAILS
- JUICY PRIME RIBS
- PLUMP LOBSTERS
- FRESH JERSEY SEA FOOD
- HOT HOME BAKED GOODS
- SPECIAL CHILDREN'S MENU

"We might just be ...

the best family restaurant in the world...

The clock from Zaberer's famous sign; Ed Zaberer loved kids and warmly welcomed them to his restaurant. Opposite: Ed meets President Richard Nixon. (Wildwood Historical Society)

Ed was nicknamed "The Host of the Coast" because he welcomed many celebrities. The walls held photographs of famous people who enjoyed dining at Zaberer's – for example Liberace, Tip O'Neill and Ronald Reagan. And always in each photo were Ed and Ayne.

Ed enjoyed speaking with the children and would pose sitting on the barber chair in the lobby with a child on his lap. He always had a treat for the kids and there was a part of the menu devoted to foods for the kids – "Ed Zaberer loves kids and kids love Ed Zaberer."

The menu was huge in size and in offerings and it was written in English and French for the French-speaking Canadian visitors. On the menu was printed: "We might just be the best family restaurant in the world." That is what Ed Zaberer wanted.

In the bar you could order one of the "Zaberized" or king-sized drinks while you were waiting for a table and then take it to your table. After you looked over the giant menu you might order Anglesea Clam Chowder and then Roast Prime Rib of Beef ("our famous large cut") or in French (Le Fameus Roti de Boeuf). And each entreé included the popular Fresh Baked Homemade Sweet Rolls and Cinnamon Buns, Butter Mold, Celery Tray, Salad with choice of dressings, and choice of potato and vegetable.

According to Ann Vinci, President of Wildwood Historical Society, "The portions were generous. The prime rib was so big it hung over the plate. The stuffed baked potatoes were large, hot and delicious. Each meal began with a basket of freshly-baked rolls, cinnamon buns and a celery tray. Those were the days!"

Bert Eisele was the reknowned pastry chef and Joseph Westog was the executive chef for many years. There were lines

around the block. Zaberer's served more than 3,000 dinners every night – 4,000 on weekends.

After operating Zaberer's for 35 years, Ed sold the business in 1987 to a New York City businessman who in 1991 held an auction of all the collections, including the Tiffany lamps... it took four days.

On June 10, 1992, someone set fire to the building. That person was never found and the building burned to the ground. It was sad to see that happen to such a great institution. Ed and Ayne moved to Pompano Beach, Florida where he died in 2001 at the age of 83.

Stuffed Baked Potatoes

A Stuffed Baked Potato was a popular choice on the Zaberer's menu. This is not an authentic recipe but I prepared a recipe as I remember the potatoes served at Zaberer's. After the potatoes are baked, the insides were removed and mashed. The filled potato was decorated using a pastry tube filled with mashed potatoes and then it was covered with grated cheese, sprinkled with paprika and put back in the oven to brown. – Anita Hirsch

6 Idaho or baking potatoes
3 tablespoons butter
3 tablespoons milk
1/8 teaspoon garlic powder
1/8 teaspoon salt
2 egg whites, stiffly beaten
2 tablespoons grated cheese
   (Parmesan, Pecorino or Cheddar)
Paprika

Wash and scrub the potatoes. Oil the potatoes with your favorite cooking oil using a pastry brush or just oil your hands and rub them over each potato. Place the potatoes on a baking sheet and bake at 425 degrees for 30 minutes. Remove the tray from the oven and pierce each potato with a fork to allow the steam to escape.

Place the tray back into the oven and bake another 20-30 minutes or until the potatoes are tender.

Allow the potatoes to cool enough to handle them. Cut a thin slice of skin off the top of each potato, wide enough so you can scoop out the insides. Place the insides of the potatoes in a bowl and place the empty skins on a baking sheet. Have the stiffly-beaten egg whites nearby. Then heat the butter and milk together in a small microwavable bowl until the butter is just melted. Beat the butter and milk mixture into the potato pulp with the garlic powder and salt. Beat until fluffy and no lumps remain. Fold the stiffly-beaten egg whites into the potato mixture.

Fill the potato skins with the potato mixture. There will be extra potato, which you can place in a pastry bag to decorate the top of the stuffed potatoes. Top each potato with about a teaspoon of the grated cheese and some paprika.

Place the potatoes back into a 400-degree oven until golden brown or place about eight inches under the broiler, just until the cheese is golden.

Tip: If you stuff the potatoes early in the day or cover and refrigerate the day before, you can heat and brown the potatoes in a 400 degree oven until brown, about 20 minutes, just before serving.

Yields six servings

Elizabeth and Joseph Russo; the restaurant they founded as it was before closing in 2008; and as it was when it was called the Gingham Club (Wildwood Historical Society)

Russo's Restaurant

86 years of home-cooked delicacies

RUSSO'S, one of the oldest restaurants in Wildwood, closed in 2008, after 86 years. Elizabeth and Joseph Russo, his brother Sam (Tootsie) and brother Ray settled in Wildwood because it reminded them of their Italian home by the Adriatic Sea. Ray opened the Golden Dragon restaurant. Elizabeth, Joseph and Tootsie bought land on the corner of Park Boulevard and Davis. They opened the Brass Rail next to the corner and started selling cold drinks and lunches to those visiting across the street at Ottens Harbor. Joe's son-in-law Santo Clement operated a drug store on the corner.

At that time, in the 1920s, Ottens Harbor was a bootleggers' hotspot. Whiskey, especially, was smuggled in – and bootleg liquor was sold in the bar at the Brass Rail.

Tootsie worked on the railroad, helping to install tracks in the evening. Until prohibition was repealed, he brought in rum to make extra money.

In the 1940s the Russos decided to expand. Joe thought the corner property would be ideal for a restaurant so they opened the Gingham Club. It had a full bar and a dining room. Delicious home-cooked style meals were served there. There was entertainment and free spaghetti nights. Entertainers appearing in local night spots would stop at the restaurant for a meal or pizza. For $2, you could get a full-course steak dinner.

In 1962, there was a hurricane and flood which damaged the Gingham

Club so they rebuilt the restaurant and then called it Russo's. They decided they should use their own name. Some who remember the Gingham Club still refer to Russo's Restaurant as the Gingham Club.

The family was important to the Russos. A family history was written on the menu and framed photos hung on the walls. A family tree was displayed prominently on the back dining room wall.

Russo's specialty was home-cooked foods. All of the Russo children and grandchildren were involved in the business at one time or another. They learned the recipes and cooking methods of mom Elizabeth. "There was always a Russo on the premises to oversee details," says her daughter, Rae Santaniello.

In 2008, Russo's was sold to Chuck Burns, who demolished the building and rebuilt it as the Ice House.

Braciole

Braciole, or beef rolls, was "the best recipe", we served says Rae Santeniello. "Guests would call before they came to see if the Braciole was on the menu that night."

In the restaurant they would make a paste of the stuffing ingredients and spread it on the beef, but Rae remembers her mom used a filling with chopped eggs and sausage. Rae advised that to get the proper cut of beef it was best to go to an Italian market and tell the butcher that you want it for Braciole.

This recipe is a family recipe from Michael Ianni, who makes a sauce and then the Braciole. Although some use top round or top sirloin cut thin, he likes to use flank steak that has been pounded to half-an-inch thick.

The recipe can be doubled.

3 cups tomato sauce (your homemade or favorite bottled sauce)
1 lb beef flank steak, pounded to half-inch thick (will measure 8" x 10")
1 1/4 cups flavored croutons (or about 6 tablespoons flavored breadcrumbs)
1/3 cup grated Parmesan cheese
2 eggs
1 tablespoon chopped fresh Italian parsley
1 tablespoon chopped fresh oregano
1 teaspoon finely chopped rosemary
1 teaspoon finely chopped thyme
2 garlic cloves, minced
Olive oil for brushing
Salt and pepper
1-2 tablespoons canola oil for searing

Preheat the oven to 350 degrees. Pour the three cups of tomato sauce in a 9 x 13 inch baking dish and place in the oven to heat.

In the bowl of food processor, combine the croutons, parmesan, eggs, parsley, oregano, rosemary, thyme and garlic until it resembles chunky bread crumbs or almost a paste. Brush the meat with olive oil and season with the salt and pepper. Spread the filling evenly over the meat. Roll tightly and tie with butchers string or hold together with wooden toothpicks.

In a large sauté pan, heat 1-2 tablespoons of canola oil. Add the roll and sear on all sides. Remove the roll from the pan and place over the hot tomato sauce in the pan in the oven. Cover with tinfoil so that the foil is not touching the meat. Bake (braise) for an hour or until tender and cooked through.

Yields four servings

Fitzharris Restaurant before it became Duffy's
(Wildwood Historical Society)

Duffy's on the Lake

Through the years, a popular gathering spot at a beautiful location

A FAVORITE restaurant since 1900, Duffy's began as a Victorian home at the corner of Pine and Atlantic Avenues in Wildwood. In 1921, the home was moved to Wildwood Crest to the corner of New Jersey and Farragut Avenues where it stands today. It was renovated and opened as Fitzharris Restaurant, where it became a popular gathering place.

Some time later, Fitzharris was bought by Ann and Joe Motley, the name was changed to Motley's Restaurant and the spot remained a popular food destination. In 1963, it was purchased by Mary and Duffy Asselta and Phyllis and John DeFranceso. Duffy was well known in the Wildwoods and very personable, so the name of the restaurant was changed to Duffy's on the Lake. The two wives had a passion for antiques and decided to furnish the dining room with many of their favorite things. The excellent reputation of the restaurant continued.

When the two families had a falling out they sold the restaurant back to Ann Motley in 1964 and she operated the restaurant until 1995. (In 1964, Mary and Duffy Asselta built and opened Duffinetti's Restaurant in Wildwood Crest.)

In 1995, the restaurant was purchased by three men – chef Jim Kurtz, Brian Burke, who is the breakfast expediter, and Billy Feraco, a silent partner and owner of Joe Canal's in Rio Grande. Chef Jim Kurtz is the son of Al Kurtz, who had owned Kurtz Restaurant at Park Boulevard and Sweet Briar Road in Wildwood Crest for many years. Jim says that he "cut his teeth at his father's restaurant."

A large and tasty menu can be enjoyed while watching the sunset over Sunset Lake. The restaurant seats 200, and once it opens for breakfast and dinner daily in season the lines are long.

The working owners of Duffy's on the Lake: left to right, chef Jim Kurtz, Eileen Burke, Brian Burke

Caesar Salad Dressing

Chef Jim Kurtz, a culinary school graduate, prepares several gallons of this dressing for the restaurant every day. It has been modified to yield two cups.

1 1/2 eggs or 4 tablespoons egg
    substitute
2 cups olive oil
1 anchovy filet chopped
1 tablespoon red wine vinegar
1 tablespoon lemon juice
1 teaspoon Worcestershire Sauce
1 1/2 teaspoons Grey Poupon mustard
1–2 cloves garlic, minced
1/4 teaspoon salt
1/8 teaspoon pepper
1–2 tablespoons grated Parmesan or
    Locatelli cheese

In a food blender or processor, beat egg or egg substitute and slowly add the olive oil until just thickened. Add the anchovy and blend.

Remove the mix to a bowl and add all the remaining ingredients except the cheese with a spoon. Finally, add the cheese.

Yields two cups

The Magnatones playing in front of the Convention Hall during a Fifties Weekend: Skip McCarty on guitar, Ed Hickman on sax, singer Jimmy (Pasquarello) Anthony and Ed Gibson on bass. Billy Zane (drummer) is hidden. Opposite, the original Magnatones: rear, from left, Billy Zane, Shawn Kelly, Ed Hickman; front, Joe Spytek, Jim Pasquarello.

The Music of the Fifties and Sixties

The Music of the Fifties and Sixties and the Magnatones

WILDWOOD in the summer, especially in the Fifties and Sixties, was the place to go to hear the best music. Many notable bands and singers could be found in the dance halls and the 31 clubs located around Oak and Atlantic Avenues, each featuring a different headliner.

Music lovers would go from club to club to hear their favorite singer or group. Ginny Wood, a Wildwood native, loved to stop at her three favorite clubs in those days: Phil and Eddie's on Schellenger near Atlantic, the Bolero, and the Rip Tide. Two other red-hot venues were the Martinique and the Oak Club.

When Bill Haley came to town with

the Comets in 1954, he played at the Hofbrau Hotel, later known as Valentino's. Two other favorite spots were the Rainbow and the Fairview, which featured Sal Masie and the Untouchables. The Fifth Dimension appeared at the Hurricane, on Pacific Avenue. Later it became Garfield's, and then Luna.

In those days the many black enter-

Bill Haley and the Comets introduced "Rock Around the Clock" to the world at the Hofbrau Hotel, a venue they regularly played. Above: New Jersey's largest bar, the Martinique Café, featured the great Louis Armstrong. Opposite: the Rainbow was one of many nightspots that attracted big names, and customers galore.
(Wildwood Historical Society)

tainers couldn't stay in the hotels and motels so they were welcomed at a large rooming house on Schellenger and New Jersey that was owned and run by Mrs Gibson. Her son Steve was the leader of Steve Gibson and the Red Caps, with Damita Joe.

The entertainers would perform in Las Vegas in the winter and come to Wildwood in the summer. Here are a few more big names who regularly played here: Paul Anka, Bobby Rydell, Ray Charles, the Shirelles, Herman's Hermits, The Grass Roots, The Crystals ("Da Do Ron Ron" and "Then He Kissed Me"), 1910 Fruitgum Company, The Rip Chords, The Monkees, The Flamingos,

Fabian, The Dovells, The Orlons, and Danny and the Juniors ("At the Hop").

The Treniers – four brothers who sang, danced, and summered in the Wildwoods – recorded "Everything's Wild in Wildwood". And there was Freddie Bell and the Bellboys, Buddy Holly's Crickets, The Drifters ("What A Wonderful World", "Under The Boardwalk", and "Take It Back!"), The Coasters ("Yackety Yack"), The Chantels, The Cadillacs, Little Anthony and the Imperials, The Dovells, Johnny Maestro and the Brooklyn Bridge, the Platters ("Only You", "Twilight Time", "Smoke Gets in Your Eyes", and "The Great Pretender"), The Shangri-Las, Joey Dee and the Starlight-

ers ("Peppermint Twist"), Tommy James and the Shondells, the Soul Survivors, the Turtles, the Beach Boy sound of "Help, Help Me Rhonda" and "California Girl", and Frankie Avalon.

Do these names and songs bring back memories?

Now many of these entertainers are coming back to Wildwood to perform during the Fabulous Fifties and Sixties Weekends. The first-ever Wildwood Music Award was given to Charlie Gracie, a Philadelphia native. He presented Chubby Checker with the second annual Wildwood Music Award in 2005.

A part of Pacific Avenue will be known as the Avenue of Fame, an idea started by Paul Russo, owner of Cool Scoops Ice Cream Parlor. Markers are inserted in the sidewalk to honor the rock and roll greats. Spicer Avenue has been renamed Chubby Checker Boulevard, because Chubby first introduced the Twist in Wildwood in 1963 at the Rainbow Supper Club on Pacific and Spicer Avenues.

Another marker was placed at the Beach Terrace Motor Inn on Atlantic Avenue, the location of the former Hofbrau Hotel, where Bill Hailey and the Comets introduced the world to "Rock Around the Clock."

"Performing in Wildwood during the 1960s was a great thrill for all of us," says Ed Hickman of The Magnatones.

The Emerald Bar was a favorite Wildwood nightspot and a regular venue for the Magnatones. Right: Charlie Gracie playing the Bolero in 1958. (Wildwood Historical Society)

"The fact that we were so young to be presented with this opportunity was even more special. All of the fans that followed us through those years and even the High Hopes, who we shared the stage with at the Emerald Room, gave us all the support we needed. From our start at the Emerald Room, all the way to Las Vegas and back again, it was a thrilling ride that could never be duplicated."

The Magnatones still play up and down the east coast, including a Fifties Weekend reunion in Wildwood in 2006.

The Magnatones originated in Gloucester City, New Jersey and all were in high school at the time, graduating in 1959. Ed Hickman played the saxophone and sang and Billy Zane played the drums and sang when they were members of the Kay-Dets. Ed was asked to join the Magnatones by Bobby Camelli, the drummer. Joey Spytek and Paul Dufay were the other original Magnatones.

They were taken under the wing of an ex-Vaudevillian Tommy Tattler, who taught them how to be professionals, including how to enter and exit the stage, how to dress and how to dance.

Tattler was the one who booked the Magnatones into the Emerald Room in Wildwood before any one in the group graduated from high school. The Emerald Room, a classy spot in Wildwood, was part of the Blackstone Hotel. The Magnatones appeared every summer, seven nights a week from Memorial Day to Labor Day, for eight years. Ed Hickman remembers celebrating the 16th birthday of Bobby McCann, the bass player at the time, in Wildwood. "We were so young! We couldn't even drink in the bars that we played in," says Ed. "Even in Las Vegas we had to be led by security up to the stage."

The current Magnatones are Ed Hickman on sax, Ed Gibson on bass, Skip McCarty on guitar, Billy Zane on drums, and the singer is Jimmy (Pasquarello) Anthony. Some of the old songs they like to play include "Splish Splash", "Bristol Stomp", "Sixteen Candles" and "In the Still of the Night".

Phil Bonelli and Eddie Rossi in front of Phil and Eddie's Surf Club (Wildwood Historical Society)

Jackie Hickman's Chicken Cutlets

Jackie Hickman whose husband Ed is part of the Magnatones, says this is an easy recipe and can be served with vegetables, used with pasta and sauce, on a sandwich or cut into strips and used in a salad.

1 lb chicken cutlets
4 tablespoons mayo, light
4 tablespoons bread crumbs
4 tablespoons grated Parmesan
    cheese

Slice each of the chicken cutlets vertically, so they will be thin. There will be about six slices. Grease or spray a baking sheet with non stick spray. Lay the chicken cutlets on the baking sheet.

Spread a layer of mayonnaise over the chicken. Then sprinkle a layer of bread crumbs over the top and finally a layer of parmesan over that.

Bake uncovered for 1 1/2 hours at 250 degrees. They should be nicely crispy on top and slightly browned. Check after an hour - they should be ready by then.

Yields three to six servings

The Starlight Ballroom

And Memories Of Dot Marsero Wadlinger

WHAT Dot Marsero Wadlinger remembers most about Wildwood summers was her first paying job... and dancing at the Starlight Ballroom.

Dot and her sister, Janet Marsero Berman, spent their summers in the 1950s with their grandparents, Vincent and Olympia Marsero, who owned a rooming house, the JanDot Hotel on Oak Avenue. Coming from the city life of Philadelphia, and always under the watchful eye of her parents, Dot welcomed the freedom she had in Wildwood.

Dot's first paying job was the summer that she was 16, when she earned a dollar an hour at Woolworth's Five & Dime on Pacific Avenue. As soon as she received her weekly pay of $36, she went across the street to the Marine National Bank, deposited $30 in her savings account and kept $6 for spending that week. By the end of the summer, Dot was able to save enough to buy a car: a 1952 Kaiser for $300.

Oak Avenue was the location of many of the clubs, but you had to be 21 years old to get into those. However, at the end of Oak at the boardwalk was the Starlight Ballroom, where Dot could go to dance. Only sodas were served at the Starlight Ballroom and it cost $1to get in. Dot remembers, "The ocean flowed right underneath the boardwalk and the Starlight Ballroom."

Every Wednesday and Saturday nights, Dot would walk up to the Starlight Ballroom. She remembers, "One of the nights was called party night." Joe Grady and Ed Hurst were the disc jockeys who "ran the dances." At the end of each night, "like a New Year's Eve party," they would play "Golden Slipper," the famous South Philly Mummers' song and then "Auld Lang Syne."

Dot still looks forward to coming to Wildwood several times each summer to dance at the clubs, but now the songs

HUNT'S Starlight
BALL ROOM
SANDWICHES
10
10
HOT DOGS
DANCING
STARLIGHT
BALLROOM
FRI SAT

she likes are called "the oldies". She especially enjoys the Fifties and Sixties weekends in Wildwood where on Friday nights Dot can dance to the oldies tunes spun by Jerry Blavat, the "Geator with the Heator" or "the Boss with the Hot Sauce".

There is a Starlight Ballroom in the new Wildwood Convention Center to honor a part of Wildwood's past. The neon sign in the lobby points to the location of the newest Starlight Ballroom.

Starlight Ballroom featured on a 1960s postcard (Wildwood Historical Society)

Jerry Blavat spins records at the 2008 Sixties Weekend

The Hunt family, who owned property and buildings in Wildwood, opened the Starlight Ballroom in Hunt's Pier in 1936. It was moved to the Ocean Pier but still kept the name. On warm summer nights, it was the place to go to dress up, to learn to jitterbug, to meet your friends, or to meet that special girl or guy. A boy would walk across the dance floor to ask a girl to dance under a spinning and sparkling globe.

The "Big Bands" appeared there: Glenn Miller, Tommy and Jimmy Dorsey, Guy Lombardo, and Woody Herman. The only big bands that DIDN'T play there

were Benny Goodman and Harry James.

A fire in the Ocean Pier Starlight Ballroom in 1943 caused the Hunt family to find another available place and they opened a Hunt's Starlight Ballroom at their pier site on Oak Avenue.

Ginny Wood, a lifelong resident of Wildwood, recollects that her father, John Wood, was in business then to refinish floors. Ginny said that he resurfaced the floor of the newest Starlight Ballroom before it opened around 1943. Her parents would take her to the Starlight to introduce her to the music and she remembers hearing Ray Charles, the

Grady and Hurst, DJs at the Starlight in the 1950s
(Wildwood Historical Society)

Shirelles, Paul Anka and the Fifth Dimension there.

One of the biggest nightclub attractions in Wildwood, Bill Haley and the Comets, returned to the Starlight in 1955 to play for Labor Day Weekend. They were the headliners for the off-season in Wildwood and made famous the song "That'll Be The Day."

After the Big Band era, the main ballroom that held 2600 was often packed with a standing room only crowd to hear records played by a DJ. It started with Bob Horn and Jerry Blavat, who was head of a Band Stand committee in Philadelphia.

Dick Clark got his start at the Starlight Ballroom – he was there for several years before he moved to Philadelphia TV.

In 1957, Grady and Hurst were the two men who played the recordings for the dancers. Later, Ron Diamond played for those who came to dance.

When Ginny Wood was a teen, she went with her friends to the Starlight almost every night in the summers. "That was the only place to go!" The Starlight Ballroom was packed with kids, who danced all night and every night. In the early Sixties "when the Bristol Stomp was popular, the floor of the Starlight Ballroom would move in waves as the dancers jumped", says Ginny. "You could feel it"!

As the music changed into hard rock or heavy metal, the kids didn't dance, and the drinking age was lowered to 18 so the older teens could go into the clubs to hear live music and dance and drink.

The Starlight Ballroom, still owned by the Hunt's family, changed too, and was made into an arcade with 12 businesses. But in 1981, a short in a wire in one of the concessions started a fire that was fanned by strong winds and burned Hunt's Starlight Ballroom to the ground.

Weeks afterward, the smell of burnt wood still lingered in the Wildwood air.

Dot Marsero Wadlinger's Risotto Milanese

When the Marseros get together in Wildwood, Dot traditionally prepares Risotto Milanese. She leaves the pot on the stove and everyone passes with a plate. First they flatten out the risotto, then cover it with grated Parmesan, and eat from around the coolest edges of the circle of rice first. It's the tradition!

2 tablespoons olive oil
2 links hot Italian sausage
1 cup chopped onions
1-2 cloves garlic, minced
1/2 teaspoon dried parsley
1/2 teaspoon dried oregano
1/2 teaspoon salt
4 cups water
1 lb Carolina brand white rice
1 (32 oz) can College Inn chicken broth
1 (8 oz) can tomato sauce
Grated Parmesan cheese

Heat oil in 2-quart heavy pot. Add sausage that has been removed from casing and crumble into the oil. Add onion and garlic and sauté until onions are soft and sausage is brown. Add parsley, oregano, salt, water. Bring to boil. Add rice. Simmer uncovered. When water is absorbed, add broth. Continue cooking uncovered for 20 minutes. Add tomato sauce. Cook another 10 minutes. Serve with cheese.

Yields 10 (3/4 cup) servings

Moore's Inlet

For 93 years, an unforgettable spot by the water

A T THE northernmost part of the five-mile island at Spruce and New Jersey Avenues was an oceanfront patio bar called Moore's Inlet. On a balmy summer night there was sure to be music coming from the main part of the building, although most people were sitting or standing outside and their cars were parked blocks away.

Charlie Gracie, the guitar player, was the headliner there for 25 years, from the early Fifties to the early Seventies when Wildwood rocked. Everyone came to see Charlie, talk to him, say hello and hear him play. His most famous song was "Butterfly", which sold more than three million copies in 1957. Charlie was a "rock-n-roll innovator" from South Philadelphia. Other famous songs from Charlie Gracie were "Fabulous", "Ninety-Nine Ways", "Wanderin' Eyes", and "I Love You So Much It Hurts." According to George Harrison, the ex-Beatle, Charlie "does brilliant guitar work."

Dot Wadlinger, who spent her teen summers in Wildwood, says, "Kids talked about going to the Penalty Box and the Stardust but the parents went to Moore's Inlet and Kenan's."

The food served at Moore's Inlet came from the corner of the building, called Janee's Kitchen. Janee was Janee Gilbert-McKee, who began waitressing at Moore's in 1982. She enjoyed it and did some cooking and soon she was asked to take over the food concession. For 13 years she operated Janee's Kitchen with her devoted seven-person crew. Her specialty was a hot roast pork sandwich with roasted peppers and onions. Some patrons liked to add provolone cheese. If you ordered the sandwich with provolone it was known as the Three Ps: Pork, Pepper and Provolone.

Moore's Inlet opened in 1912 and closed its doors 93 years later. The last owners were Mike Guagadno and Joe Bilbee, who was the nightly DJ. In 2005,

Moore's Inlet was torn down and 60 luxury condominiums called The Pointe at Moore's Inlet were built.

"Olde Lang Syne"

James L. Shelton of Wildwood Crest was moved to write a poem about the loss of Moore's Inlet. Here is part of his poem that appeared as a Letter to the Editor in the *Wildwood Leader* on September 21, 2005.

*They came in droves for the spring fling
And stayed till Labor Day.
Always rejoicing together in the perpetual
Motion the melodies played by
The Legendary disc jockey Joe Bilbee,
And the variety pack of sounds, humor
And happy countenance of the
Talented Tony Mascara.*

*They came to be greeted by the friendly
And gracious owner Mike Guadagno,
They came to be serviced by the finest
Group of bartenders anywhere,*

*The indefatigable "Boo" and Sticks,
Marty Boots,
Al, Jim, Freddie, Danny and Mark,
They came to enjoy good food from Janee's
Kitchen, served by the bevy of beautiful
And smiling wait staff,
Laurie, Kim, Jess, Kate, Marie, Patrice,
Tom and Tim and Melissa.
And of course we were always protected
From trouble by the young brigade of*

*Gentlemen Joe, JJ, Timmy, Pat, Bryan, Doc,
And the effervescent "Hank."
And perhaps if you were lucky
You might have had your picture taken by
The charming and beautiful Jamie.*

*Moore's Inlet has become a home away
From home,
A brief summer respite from the
Crowded highways they have to drive over
Each day of their lives,
Their busy schedules, tired commitments
From the pain of some of their relationships
From economic hardship
And from a world always seemingly on the
Verge of collapse!*

*But once here
In the safety net of this
Friendly bar and restaurant
They relaxed
They danced
They drank...
They found acceptance
Friendship...*

Pictured clockwise from left: Kim Stocks, waitress at Moore's for 20 years; bartender Al Trottnow worked at Moore's for 26 years; Joe Urzillo and Frank McGugan, members of the Avalon String Band, take time out at Moore's Inlet; Paul Hatterty, tending bar outside at Moore's Inlet, where he worked for 31 years; Charlie Gracie playing the guitar at Moore's.

Janee's Kitchen
Three Ps Sandwich

A popular sandwich at Moore's Inlet was the Three Ps Sandwich: Pork, Pepper and Provolone. This recipe was developed to taste like that original sandwich; this recipe is not Janee's but one that hopefully tastes as good as the one prepared in Janee's Kitchen. – Anita Hirsch

1 lb boneless pork tenderloin or loin, cut into thin strips
1/4 cup reduced fat Italian dressing
1/2 medium onion, sliced
1 cup sliced bell pepper (green, red, and/or yellow)
1/2 teaspoon garlic powder
2 tablespoons lemon juice
8 slices provolone
4 (8-inch) steak rolls

In a heavy plastic bag, mix pork strips and dressing. Refrigerate several hours or overnight. Drain liquid. Heat a 12-inch nonstick skillet over medium-high heat; stir-fry pork and onions for 5 minutes. Stir in peppers and cook five more minutes. Add garlic powder and lemon juice; toss to coat.

Cut warm steak rolls, add 2 slices of provolone along the open cut. Add a quarter of the pork, onion and pepper mixture and serve. Prepare 3 more sandwiches.

Yields four sandwiches

Acknowledgments

I AM indebted to so many who helped me with this book. First Dorothy Kulisek, the editor of the *Sun-by-the-Sea,* who designed the cover, encouraged me to finish the book, and shared her photos and her memories. Thank you to the Wildwood Historical Society, especially Bob Bright, Anne Vinci and Robert J. Scully Sr, who were supportive and welcoming. Thanks to Jack Wright for his unrelenting energy level in getting out this book. Thanks to everyone who spoke to me and shared stories and family photographs.

I also want to thank Ernie Troiano Sr, Pete DiGiannantonio, Ann Silvidio Suppa, Angelo Pantelone, Nina Marsero Finnegan, Joe Gallagher, Ashley Weigle, Chuck Schumann, Harry and Coleen DiSilvestro, Barbara Flacco and Marie Donohue. Thanks to Ralph Grassi and his wonderful website www.Funchase.com. Thanks to Mary and Mike Baklycki, Ralph Catanese and Dave Callen for contributing to the Wildwood Crest Fishing Pier story.

For information about Duffy's on the Lake, I thank Sue Tull, Jana DeFrancesco, and Eileen Burke.

Thank you to Theresa and David Williams from the Wildwood Crest Historical Museum who gave me much time and many photographs. Thanks to my neighbors on Bennett Avenue who were always there to answer questions: Josephine Daning, Al and Diane Brannon, Gary and Janet Berman. Thanks to Nancy Bailey for suggestions and copy-editing assistance. Thanks to Brenda Bortz, a great creative influence and to Aleksey Moryakov for being available for last-minute photo shoots and to Rob Kulisek for his photographic eye.

Other resources I found valuable were:
Wildwood: The Middle of the Island by George F. Boyer, Laureate Press, 1976.

History of Philip Pontius Baker compiled by Kirk Hastings in the Wildwood Crest Historical Museum.

Wildwood-by-the-Sea by David Francis, Diane D. Francis and Robert Scully, Sr. for information about the Ship Ahoy Motel.

Wildwoodhistory.org by Maureen Cawley

Finally, I would like to thank Maxine Hirsch for all her help. I thank Sy and Leanne, who were very patient, kept me focused, and were always willing to stop while I took photos. And to Michael for his encouragement and advice, and for always taking the time to shoot photographs and to share his own.

Index

About the Author

A Registered Dietitian with a Master's degree from Rutgers University in New Jersey, Anita Hirsch taught as an adjunct professor at the College of St. Elizabeth in Morristown, New Jersey. She has written for Rodale publications and is a columnist for the popular Wildwood publication *Sun-by-the-Sea*. This is her sixth book. Contact Anita at tasteofwildwood@aol.com.

Wildwood Crest Fishing Pier (Wildwood Historical Society)